Leonardo, Michelangelo and Raphael: The Greatest Artists of the Renaissance

By Charles River Editors

Leonardo's design of a helicopter, from his notebooks

Introduction

Leonardo's self-portrait, circa 1512

Leonardo da Vinci (1452-1519)

"Iron rusts from disuse; stagnant water loses its purity and in cold weather becomes frozen; even so does inaction sap the vigor of the mind." – Leonardo

The Renaissance also spawned the use of the label "Renaissance Man" to describe a person who is extremely talented in multiple fields, and no discussion of the Renaissance is complete without the original "Renaissance Man", Leonardo da Vinci. Indeed, if 100 people are asked to describe Leonardo in one word, they might give 100 answers. As the world's most famous polymath and genius, Leonardo found time to be a painter, sculptor, architect, musician, scientist, mathematician, engineer, inventor, anatomist, geologist, cartographer, botanist, and writer.

It would be hard to determine which field Leonardo had the greatest influence in. His "Mona Lisa" and "The Last Supper" are among the most famous paintings of all time, standing up against even Michelangelo's work. But even if he was not the age's greatest artist, Leonardo may have conducted his most influential work was done in other fields. His emphasis on the importance of Nature would influence Enlightened philosophers centuries later, and he sketched speculative designs for gadgets like helicopters that would take another 4 centuries to create. Leonardo's vision and philosophy were made possible by his astounding work as a mathematician, engineer and scientist. At a time when much of science was dictated by Church teachings, Leonardo studied geology and anatomy long before they truly even became scientific fields, and he used his incredible artistic abilities to sketch the famous Vitruvian Man, linking art and science together.

Leonardo also conducted scientific experiments using empirical methods nearly 150 years before Rene Descartes' "Discourse on Method." As Leonardo explained in his writings, "Many will think they may reasonably blame me by alleging that my proofs are opposed to the authority of certain men held in the highest reverence by their inexperienced judgments; not considering that my works are the issue of pure and simple experience, who is the one true mistress."

Leonardo, Michelangelo and Raphael chronicles Leonardo's amazing life and work, analyzing the lasting legacy he left across the arts and sciences. Along with pictures of important people, places, and events in his life, you will learn about Leonardo like never before.

Portrait of Michelangelo by Jacopino del Conte, circa 1535

Michelangelo (1475-1564)

"If people knew how hard I had to work to gain my mastery, it would not seem so wonderful at all." – Michelangelo

It's possible that Michelangelo is the most famous artist in history, but it's also possible that he's an underrated artist. The vast influence of his career is reflected by the fact that he is not only known for his own art but has also come to embody an entire epoch of Western art. Along with Leonardo da Vinci, there are no other artists who so fully capture the spirit of scientific and artistic discovery that characterized art during the late 15th and early 16th centuries. Moreover, Michelangelo's career is distinguished from that of his peers through his seamless ability to work within different art forms, receiving acclaim regardless of the medium. After first rising to fame as a sculptor, he also painted and served as an architect, and since his death, Michelangelo has also become decorated for his prolific output as a poet. The diversity and high standard of his work, no matter the medium, make it difficult to even arrive at a most famous work. People can make a compelling argument for at least three works: the statue of David (1501-1504), the ceiling of the Sistine Chapel (1508-1512), or the design for St. Peter's Basilica (worked on from 1546 through his death). That the same artist produced these canonical monuments of Western art is remarkable, but that each was made through a different medium defines Michelangelo as a sui generis talent.

To top it off, Michelangelo's work came at the height of a period in Western civilization known for its scientific and artistic exploration. As Michelangelo biographer George Bull noted, this period carries many titles: "The period of Michelangelo's lifetime has been variously characterized as the age of printing, the age of humanism, the Reformation, Counter-Reformation, Catholic Reform, the waning of the Middle Ages, the Renaissance, and the age of Discovery." The different titles reflect the sheer amount of activity that took place during this critical era of Western Civilization. Although the different labels can frustrate attempts to clearly define the era, each one of them is important to remember in the context of Michelangelo's career.

Leonardo, Michelangelo and Raphael chronicles the famous artist's life and work, as well as his lasting legacy. Along with pictures of important people, places, and events in his life, you will learn about Michelangelo like never before.

Raphael's self-portrait (1506)

Raphael (1483-1520)

"Here lies that famous Raphael by whom Nature feared to be conquered while he lived, and when he was dying, feared herself to die." – Inscription on Raphael's sarcophagus

Raffaello Sanzio da Urbino, known across the world simply by the name Raphael, stands as one of the main pillars of the High Renaissance, an iconic example of the balance between spirituality and Humanistic inquiry that characterized the time period. Although he lived just 37 years, his career produced an amazingly rich output, and he completed more works than many artists do over careers spanning twice the length. At the same time, Raphael's art combined central tropes associated with the Renaissance while remaining remarkably original. As such, his career is not only worth exploring in its own right, but also for the ways in which he typified contemporary artistic techniques, including a return to antiquity and the balance between mathematical accuracy, rational thought, and religious devotion.

While Raphael's own themes did not vary greatly throughout his career, he led a relatively nomadic existence, and his life reflects the trends associated with late 15th century and early 16th century Italy. Born in Umbria and raised in the Umbria court, Raphael was exposed to a wealth of artistic influences and high culture, characteristic of the early Renaissance shift toward humanism and artistic appreciation. Although Raphael's talent was generational, his life did not involve the extreme poverty and destitution that often characterized the lives of other famous artists. This ensured Raphael's life represents a useful rubric through which to examine the cultural norms of the era.

Although Raphael was perhaps the most favored artist of the Italian Renaissance, his reputation has since been surpassed by famous contemporaries like Leonardo da Vinci and Michelangelo. To this day, it is difficult to think of Raphael without considering his artistic rivals, and comparing the artwork between Raphael and his contemporaries illuminates Raphael's artistic style and the reception surrounding his work. In many ways, his art synthesized the styles of other artists; Raphael's artwork was not produced in a vacuum, and his career reflects the rise of the artist as a culturally significant figure while also preserving the grandeur of the church. Even if he lacked the innovation of Leonardo or Michelangelo, Raphael was every bit as renowned during the time period, and an analysis of his life explains his mass appeal and cultural significance.

Leonardo, Michelangelo and Raphael chronicles the famous artist's life and work, as well as his lasting legacy. Along with pictures of important people, places, and events in his life, you will learn about Raphael like never before.

Statue of Leonardo in Amboise, France

Leonardo

Chapter 1: Leonardo's Childhood

"Seeing that I can find no subject specially useful or pleasing— since the men who have come before me have taken for their own every useful or necessary theme— I must do like one who, being poor, comes last to the fair, and can find no other way of providing himself than by taking all the things already seen by other buyers, and not taken but refused by reason of their lesser value. I, then, will load my humble pack with this despised and rejected merchandise, the refuse of so many buyers; and will go about to distribute it, not indeed in great cities, but in the poorer towns, taking such a price as the wares I offer may be worth." – The Notebooks of Leonardo da Vinci

Leonardo's childhood home in Anchiano

On April 15, 1452, Lionardo di ser Piero da Vinci was born out of wedlock in or around Vinci, Italy to a relatively wealthy local notary, Ser Piero, and a young peasant woman, Caterina. Though nobody knew what the child would become, Ser Piero's father Antonio noted the birth and baptism in his daily journal.

While little is known about his early childhood, Leonardo likely remained with his mother for at least his first year of life and may have spent his first several years with her. Leonardo's mother, Caterina, eventually married another man and moved away from the area, at which point Leonardo may have been taken in by his paternal family while still an infant or as a small child. Antonio's tax records record an illegitimate five-year-old child in the household in 1457, quite likely Leonardo.

Whatever the case, Leonardo was raised by his father and stepmother in Vinci, along with his paternal grandparents, and he was treated unusually well for an illegitimate child as he was recognized and acknowledged by his father. It probably helped that Leonardo had no siblings on his father's side until he was an adult.

Leonardo was educated at home until he was 14, with his stepmother Donna Albiera and grandmother Monna Lucia managing his education. As a boy, he was taught reading, writing, and mathematics, and though a Latin teacher was employed, Leonardo never mastered Latin or Greek. Eventually, his knowledge of classical sources would come primarily from Italian translations, as well as conversations with friends and colleagues, and he did have access to a number of books in the libraries and collections of friends and family members as a child. For those reasons, it can be safely assumed Leonardo was well-read. According to his near-contemporaneous biographer Vasari, "He would have been very proficient in his early lessons, if he had not been so volatile and flexible; for he was always setting himself to learn a multitude of things, most of which were shortly abandoned. When he began the study of arithmetic, he made, within a few months, such remarkable progress that he could baffle his master with the questions and problems that he raised… All the time, through all his other enterprises, Leonardo never ceased drawing…"

When Leonardo was a teenager, the family moved to a rented home in Florence, though the property in Vinci remained in the family. By the 1460s, Florence was a lively and thriving city under the control of Lorenzo de Medici, a passionate patron of the arts who supported many artists. Lorenzo's court contributed to the creation of many of the works of the fifteenth century Italian Renaissance, including those by Ficino, Botticelli, and Michelangelo. Lorenzo followed the traditions and practices started by his grandfather, Cosimo de Medici, who had helped to support the work of Brunelleschi, Donatello and Ghiberti. While Cosimo had been well-liked by the people of Florence, Lorenzo is widely credited as being the one who anchored the Renaissance in Florence during his rule. When he died in 1492, his son Piero would rule for only two years thanks to the French invasion of Tuscany, which forced Florence's leaders to leave the city. With that, the center of the Italian Renaissance became Rome.

Lorenzo de Medici

As a boy in the city, Leonardo likely attended civic festivals held by "Lorenzo the Magnificent" and had the opportunity to see significant works of early Renaissance art and architecture. Lorenzo's court enjoyed these lavish entertainments and relied on grand artistic commissions to illustrate his wealth and power. He also brought works of classical art, including sculptures to the city. At the same time, though these many festivals were held for the people of the city, Lorenzo's wealth came from the people and his lavish lifestyle caused substantial resentments, particularly in the well-off merchant classes in Florence.

Meanwhile, young Leonardo's artistic skill was already apparent, according to art historian and painter Vasari. At around 15 years old, Leonardo was apprenticed to Andrea di Cione, known as Verrocchio. Vasari states that Ser Piero showed Leonardo's early artwork to Verrocchio and he was so impressed that he immediately accepted Leonardo into his workshop. Career options were somewhat limited for an illegitimate child, but this was, nonetheless, a highly desirable apprenticeship position. Verrocchio was a well-known artist in Florence, and his workshop would provide an ideal learning environment for the young Leonardo.

Leonardo's earliest known drawing, the Arno Valley (1473), Uffizi

Chapter 2: Apprenticeship

"Poor is the pupil that does not surpass his master." – The Notebooks of Leonardo da Vinci

Verrocchio's Tobias and the Angel Raphael

Verrocchio was a court sculptor, painter and goldsmith, but his studio also produced fine musical instruments, and Verrocchio's apprentices had the opportunity to learn all of these skills and experiment with various media. As an apprentice, Leonardo's responsibilities would have grown with time. Initially, he would have worked as a sort of servant, fetching and carrying materials, and then he would have assisted in preparing pigments, cleaning brushes and performing other tasks for the master. He would have learned to mix paints and glazes during this phase of his apprenticeship.

During the initial stages of the apprenticeship, Verrocchio would have also taken time to teach various artistic skills, which for Leonardo meant the opportunity to gain knowledge that built upon his natural talents. In the later years of his apprenticeship, he would have assisted with the creation of various works. In at least one of Verrocchio's works, there is a finely painted angel attributed to Leonardo. While in Verrocchio's workshop, Leonardo learned to sculpt and paint, make jewelry and other ornaments, and even developed a fair understanding of weaponry and cannons, a reflection of the fact that court artists were expected to be versatile and capable of handling any task set before them. In addition to his most famous pupil, Verrocchio also trained other well-respected artists, including Sandro Botticelli, Perugino and Ghirlandaio. While Verrocchio himself is not considered one of the geniuses of the Renaissance, his influence on the next generation is undeniable.

The Baptism of Christ (1472–1475)—Uffizi, by Verrocchio and Leonardo

Verrocchio is best known for his life-size and larger sculptures, including Christ and St. Thomas in the Church of Orsanmichele in Florence and the statue of the young David, dating to between 1473 and 1475. David is rumored to have been modeled on the young Leonardo da Vinci. The most famous work by Verrocchio is a large equestrian piece in Venice, the statue of Bartolomeo Colleoni, dating to 1488. While Verrocchio produced the wax models and the molds for this work, he did not live to see it completed.

As was standard for the time, most of the paintings attributed to Verrocchio are workshop pieces, meaning they were worked on in large part by his numerous apprentices. In comparison to Leonardo's work, Verrocchio's paintings are rather flat, but they do employ the perspective characteristic of Italian Renaissance art. Filippo Brunelleschi is often credited as the first to employ the perspective technique, in which artists paint the subject at the angle from which the artist sees it. Thus, instead of having the painting's subjects perfectly centered, the perspective style often places subjects off center, and the size of objects decreases in proportion to how far away from the viewer they appear. To fully accomplish this, Renaissance artists mixed colors and used lighting and shading to produce a more three-dimensional appearance, while angling subjects closer or farther away with a technique called foreshortening. In his Notebooks, Leonardo noted, "Drawing is based upon perspective, which is nothing else than a thorough knowledge of the function of the eye."

Since apprentices worked on paintings and art attributed to the master, historians and scholars often try to determine which works might have actually been done by which pupils. It's known that Leonardo contributed to Verrocchio's Baptism of Christ, and The Annunciation of Christ, largely attributed to Leonardo, although not his work alone, also dates from the period of his apprenticeship between 1472 and 1475. Still, Leonardo did not gain the skills and experience to produce large works, particularly frescoes, during his apprenticeship.

In 1472, Leonardo appears in the rolls of the painter's guild in Florence, the Compagnia di San Luca. According to Vasari, Verrocchio swore to never paint again when his pupil surpassed his skills, but this statement has little basis in fact. Leonardo's apprenticeship and official position in Verrocchio's household continued at least until 1476, and eventually, while working in Verrocchio's workshop, Leonardo learned some of the underpainting techniques he employed throughout his career.

Following the end of his apprenticeship, it is known that Leonardo remained in Florence for a number of years, though there are only a few pieces of artwork surviving from these years. An incomplete altarpiece showing the Adoration of the Magi from the Convent of St. Donato, Leonardo's first independent commission, is in the Uffuzi Gallery in Florence. There are written records of several other commissions dating to the Florentine period, and he worked on a number of pieces. The incomplete altarpiece and Benois Madonna date to this period in Leonardo's career. While the altarpiece of The Adoration of the Magi is not finished, it already illustrates

Leonardo's strong interest in realism and willingness to change the traditional iconography of a religious scene. Typically, the Adoration of the Magi is portrayed with the Magi surrounding the Christ child in the manger. Leonardo's composition places the Magi around the Virgin and Child. His Adoration was influenced by the work of a northern artist, Rogier van der Weyden, and the composition bears a distinct resemblance to Van der Weyden's Entombment of Christ, now in the Uffuzi Gallery.

The Adoration of the Magi

Though he had been trained as an artist, it's quite likely that Leonardo studied a variety of subjects during these years and may have completed his first dissections while in Florence. His later notebooks reveal sketches, writing and studies across a wide range of disciplines, and his varied interests had begun in childhood and remained a vital part of his personal and professional life. He may also have begun to design large scale military projects during his time in Florence.

While Leonardo was occasionally criticized for his academic study and failure to complete works, a single personal scandal marred his reputation. In 1476 he was accused of sodomy, along with a well-known male prostitute. Two trials resulted, but Leonardo was not convicted of the charges. Biographers vary as to the validity of these charges, but Leonardo himself maintained that he was not sexually active throughout his life and his notebooks indicate revulsion at heterosexual intercourse. There is, however, minimal contemporary evidence, outside of the records of these trials, that Leonardo maintained homosexual relationships during this stage of his life. When charged, Leonardo was still in Verrocchio's household and studio.

Leonardo was never made his father's heir, and in 1476 he was no longer his father's only child after the birth of a sibling that year. His apprenticeship also officially ended that year. Leonardo may have lived in the household of Lorenzo de Medici before leaving the city of Florence. Lorenzo's patronage was essential for a young artist's success, and he favored the young artist, allowing him to work with some classical sculptures in the piazza of San Marco. Leonardo later wrote that the "Medici created me and destroyed me".

As a young man, Leonardo was appreciated not just for his artistic talent but for a wide range of skills. He was considered to have an especially fine singing voice, and by all accounts he was an attractive young man and physically well-built, perhaps contributing to the suggestion that he was a model for Verrocchio's David. It has also been speculated that one of the figures in the background of the Adoration of the Magi may be a self-portrait of Leonardo. Contemporary records suggest that he was kind-hearted, buying birds at the market and setting them free and preferring to eat vegetarian meals rather than consuming meat.

Chapter 3: Milan

"Wisdom is the daughter of experience." – The Notebooks of Leonardo

In 1482 or 1483, Leonardo himself wrote the ruling family of Milan, the Sforzas. He was in search of a new patron and a fresh start outside of Florence. At the time, the Duke of Milan, Ludovico Sforza, held power over the city through his nephew, having brought an end to his sister's regency to gain power in Milan. The boy, Gian, was not competent to rule on his own. Sforza, called Il Moro, became Duke in his own right in 1494 when Gian died, after offering an enormous dowry and his niece to the Holy Roman Emperor Maximilien. He hoped very much to create power in Milan that could compete with the Medici family in Florence and the papal estates in Rome. Creating a court of equal social and artistic standing would thus serve to assert Il Moro's power over the state of Milan.

Sforza

Leonardo wrote to the Duke:

"Most Illustrious Lord: Having now sufficiently seen and considered the proofs of all those who count themselves masters and inventors in the instruments of war, "Most Illustrious Lord: Having now sufficiently seen and considered the proofs of all those who count themselves masters and inventors in the instruments of war, and finding that their invention and use does not differ in any respect from those in common practice, I am emboldened… to put myself in communication with your Excellency, in order to acquaint you with my secrets. I can construct bridges which are very light and strong and very portable with which to pursue and defeat an enemy… I can also make a kind of cannon, which is light and easy of transport, with which to hurl small stones like hail… I can noiselessly construct to any prescribed point subterranean passages — either straight or winding — passing if necessary under trenches or a river… I can make armored wagons carrying artillery, which can break through the most serried ranks of the enemy. In time of peace, I believe I can give you as complete satisfaction as anyone else in the construction of buildings, both public and private, and in conducting water from one place to another. I can execute sculpture in bronze, marble or clay. Also, in painting, I can do as much as anyone, whoever he may be. If any of the aforesaid things should seem impossible or impractical to anyone, I offer myself as ready to make a trial of them in your park or in whatever place shall please your Excellency, to whom I commend myself with all possible humility."

Leonardo offered his skills, but his letter was clearly not focused on his artistic abilities. Milan was threatened by a number of enemies, including the city of Venice, the papacy in Rome and the armies of France. Milan was at high risk for attack and needed both strong offenses and defenses. Thus, he promoted his skills as a military and civil engineer, as well as an architect. He went on to praise his own design abilities, stating that if cannons were unacceptable or were not needed, he could produce designs unlike any seen elsewhere. While his first military drawings appear in extant manuscripts in 1489, it seems likely that Leonardo had already begun work on military projectiles and other weapons while he lived in Florence. The 1489 drawings show devices that could be the precursor to poison gas, tanks, and smoke screens, and these were obviously the result of significant thought and research. Ultimately, none of Leonardo's military designs were produced.

It was only in the last paragraph of his letter that Leonardo mentioned his skill as a sculptor and painter. He said that he could "execute statues in marble, bronze and clay," and that he could paint "as well as anyone else". The Duke of Milan was planning a large sculpture of a horse to honor his father and had been seeking a qualified sculptor for some time. Leonardo recommended himself for this work, but he was primarily hoping for military and civil engineering projects.

Leonardo's letter was successful, though not for the reasons he had primarily hoped it would be. It's likely that Leonardo was assisted by the strong recommendation of Lorenzo de Medici, and he may have carried gifts from Lorenzo to Ludovico Sforza. Alliances were critical during this period, particularly with the military threats faced by various Italian city-states. Moreover, Ludovico's family had gained control of Milan following a military victory, but had done so with the aid of Lorenzo's grandfather, Cosimo de Medici. Thus, with Sforza's support and approval, Leonardo moved to Milan in the early 1480s, where he would remain for the next 17 years. While he had promoted his military skills, Sforza was more interested in his potential as an artist and musician. Ironically, though he later wrote, "Many are they who have a taste and love for drawing, but no talent; and this will be discernible in boys who are not diligent and never finish their drawings with shading", Leonardo had completed relatively few works in Florence. Still, even his unfinished pieces were praised.

Leonardo brought a silver lute shaped like a horse's head with him and was noted for his musical skill, frequently playing for the Duke. Sforza wished to be seen as Lorenzo de Medici's equal, complete with the finest court artists and poets, and Leonardo helped that image by designing grand festivals for the Duke and even serving as a master of ceremonies. These festivals ranged from relatively small affairs exclusively for Milan's elite to large festivals open to the general population in the city. Extant sketches and notes reveal his plans for stage sets for these festivals. Particularly in his first years in the city, while he was still quite young, he also participated in a variety of athletic contests associated with the festivities.

The Virgin of the Rocks

   Leonardo's first work in Milan was The Virgin of the Rocks, a painting that is still housed in the Louvre today. This painting was the centerpiece of a three part or triptych altarpiece, painted for the Confraternity of the Immaculate Conception in Milan. Leonardo's composition is worked in oil paints on a prepared wooden panel, rather than a canvas, while the two side panels, depicting angels, were assigned to other painters. The subject is the adoration of the Christ child by the infant John the Baptist. The image, consisting of the Virgin Mary, Elizabeth, the mother of John the Baptist and the two infants, is placed in front of a background of dramatic rocks.

   While some religious scenes were commonly painted with a grotto or cave backdrop, the rocks in the Virgin of the Rocks were quite unusual. The painting has a complex composition and shows a number of characteristics typical to Leonardo's later work, including a distinctly triangular shape. Leonardo's triangular composition was also seen in the unfinished Florentine

Adoration of the Magi, perhaps indicative of what Leonardo was talking about when he wrote, "All objects transmit their image to the eye in pyramids."

The Virgin in this painting is the first mature woman in a surviving painting by Leonardo. Contract negotiations led to a second version of the same painting, and both paintings were oil paintings worked on a wooden surface. Today, one version is in the National Gallery in London and the other in the Louvre.

Later in the 1480s, he worked on Portrait of a Musician and Lady with an Ermine. These pieces are significantly smaller than the large altarpiece. He would maintain a pattern of work on a larger public commission and a few smaller portraits at a time throughout his career. This relatively limited amount of artistic output enabled him to focus on his other intellectual interests, but he continued to leave many works unfinished.

Portrait of a Musician

As Leonardo was settling in at Milan, plague struck in 1484 and 1485. The "Black Death", bubonic plague, had been active in Northern Italy since around 1477, but 484 and 1485 were especially bad years. While the cause and spread of plague was not understood, Leonardo did realize that overcrowding and poor sanitation contributed to disease.

After the plague had come to an end, taking approximately 50,000 lives and fully one-third of the population of Milan, Leonardo created a new design for the city itself. Leonardo envisioned a city with an upper and lower level of wide roads, in which the upper level provided safe space for foot traffic while the lower level accommodated carriages and carts. Canals enabled the easy transportation of goods and provided for the management of sewage, and attractive buildings with large arcades would edge the streets. Each building included not only windows, but a ventilation system to allow access to ample fresh air. Well-designed stables provided comfortable and sanitary housing for horses. Leonardo placed this designed city near a clean water source, for drinking water and irrigation.

Leonardo did not imagine a single large city, but rather ten smaller cities to accommodate adequate sanitation and relieve overcrowding. While Leonardo created a plan that might have provided for a safe and clean home and an example for the remainder of Europe, Sforza never implemented any of Leonardo's city plans.

Between 1487 and 1490, Leonardo worked on the completion of the city cathedral from his nearby home in Milan, making drawings and designs for the domed crossing tower, as did other prominent architects of the time, including Bramante. Ultimately, the Duomo of Milan was, like many other projects, left incomplete; Leonardo built a wooden model during his attempts at design but did not take the work any further. The final domed crossing tower was designed by Milanese architects Amadeo and Dolcebuono.

Nevertheless, during his work on the cathedral Leonardo repeatedly visited the library and university at Pavia to look at architectural studies and expand his understanding of engineering. His visits to Pavia allowed him to broaden his own studies on anatomy and other subjects. He also considered and began work on models for the large equestrian statue discussed in that first letter to Sforza, which might have been Sforza's primary goal when he brought Leonardo to Milan. Though he wrote in his notebooks, "Of the horse I will say nothing because I know the times", Leonardo had already made many sketches of horses and dissected a number of specimens, providing detailed knowledge of the structure and musculature. He planned the largest work in bronze done during the Italian renaissance. The finished horse would stand 20 feet tall and weigh as much as 20,000 pounds. He worked on models and molds of the statue, but never completed it. A clay version was displayed, but later used for target practice by the French in 1499. He continued his work on this project into the 1490s; however, in 1489, the Florentine ambassador in Milan wrote to Lorenzo de Medici asking him to send sculptors. While the ambassador may have questioned the completion of the statue, the court poet celebrated the clay version and Leonardo's skill. The bronze intended for the giant statue was made into cannons for the Milanese army in 1494. It would be another 500 years before the equestrian statue as designed by Leonardo was attempted.

Leonardo's design for the equestrian statue

While Leonardo was devoted to his work, he did maintain his own household, and it was a luxurious one at that. Leonardo maintained horses, carriages, servants and a fine home, so naturally he frequently struggled with financial worries, particularly since he did not complete many of his commissions. Several letters requested payment of his salary or other financial assistance from Sforza, since he was, for his role as court artist, owed a regular salary. In 1499, Sforza, who was apparently quite financially drained himself, gave Leonardo a large vineyard near Milan as payment for his debts.

Personal changes occurred in Leonardo's life in the early 1490s. A young boy, Gian Giacomo Caprotti da Oreno, called Salai, entered the household, and he would remain with Leonardo until the end of the artist's life and was provided for in his will. The exact nature of the relationship between Leonardo and Salai is unclear, especially considering Leonardo described him as "a thief, a liar, stubborn, and a glutton" but nevertheless doted on him. Only a few works by Salai, painted under the name Andrea Salai, survived, and his Mona Vanna is so similar to the Mona Lisa that some speculate it may have been based on a lost nude by Leonardo. Salai may also have been the model for Leonardo's John the Baptist and an image of a sexually aroused angel. Several sketches in Leonardo's notebooks imply an intimate relationship. Salai accompanied Leonardo to France, and when the Renaissance Man died, he bequeathed the Mona Lisa to Salai, who went on to prepare Leonardo's writings for publication and described him as "like an excellent father to me", asserting, "Everyone is grieved at the loss of such a man that Nature no longer has it in her power to produce."

Salai

Though the extent of his relationship with Salai is unclear, relationships like that and Leonardo's own writings have long led to speculation that he was homosexual and/or celibate. While Leonardo's sexuality is trivial when discussing his accomplishments, his writings make clear that he found heterosexual sex abhorrent, writing, "The act of procreation and anything that has any relation to it is so disgusting that human beings would soon die out if there were no pretty faces and sensuous dispositions." In Leonardo's time, homosexuality was so widely accepted that the word Florenzer (Florentine) became slang for homosexual in Germany. Leonardo's painting of John the Baptist has long been cited as proof of his sexual interest in men because of its similarities to The Incarnate Angel, a charcoal sketch from his workshop of a nude, sexually excited male angel, but art scholars have speculated that it was one of Leonardo's pupils who sketched The Incarnate Angel based on Leonardo's John the Baptist, not the other way around.

John the Baptist

While historians continue to debate his sexuality, contemporary accounts all describe a handsome and athletic individual who was about 5'8. Portraits of Leonardo, including his self-portrait, indicate that he had long hair and a flowing beard as an older man, unusual for his times, and contemporaries described his clothing as eclectic and bright. Even in his older days, Leonardo preferred to wear short tunics, the choice of younger men. These characteristics were used to create the statue of Leonardo that stands outside the Uffizi Gallery.

Varsari wrote very glowingly of Leonardo, "In the normal course of events many men and women are born with various remarkable qualities and talents; but occasionally, in a way that transcends nature, a single person is marvelously endowed by heaven with beauty, grace and talent in such abundance that he leaves other men far behind…Everyone acknowledged that this was true of Leonardo da Vinci, an artist of outstanding physical beauty who displayed infinite grace in everything he did and who cultivated his genius so brilliantly that all problems he studied were solved with ease. He possessed great strength and dexterity; he was a man of regal spirit and tremendous breadth of mind…"

Leonardo apparently had the personality to match the appearance too. Varsari wrote, "Leonardo's disposition was so lovable that he commanded everyone's affection…In appearance he was striking and handsome, and his magnificent presence brought comfort to the most troubled soul; he was so persuasive that he could bend other people to his will. He was physically so strong that he could withstand violence and with his right hand he could bend the ring of an iron door knocker or a horseshoe as if they were lead. He was so generous that he fed all his friends, rich or poor…. Through his birth Florence received a very great gift, and through his death it sustained an incalculable loss."

Another characteristic of Leonardo that his contemporaries found so fascinating was how he treated animals. Though he clearly studied anatomy and participated in dissections, he seemed to hate animal cruelty so much that it made him a vegetarian. As Edward MacCurdy, who edited Leonardo's notebooks, noted, "The mere idea of permitting the existence of unnecessary suffering, still more that of taking life, was abhorrent to him. Vasari tells, as an instance of his love of animals, how when in Florence he passed places where birds were sold he would frequently take them from their cages with his own hand, and having paid the sellers the price that was asked would let them fly away in the air, thus giving them back their liberty. That this horror of inflicting pain was such as to lead him to be a vegetarian is to be inferred from a reference which occurs in a letter sent by Andrea Corsali to Giuliano di Lorenzo de' Medici, in which, after telling him of an Indian race called Gujerats who neither eat anything that contains blood nor permit any injury to any living creature, he adds 'like our Leonardo da Vinci.'"

In his Notebooks, Leonardo wrote about the subject, "If you are as you have described yourself the king of the animals — it would be better for you to call yourself king of the beasts since you are the greatest of them all! — why do you not help them so that they may presently be able to give you their young in order to gratify your palate, for the sake of which you have tried to make yourself a tomb for all the animals? Even more I might say if to speak the entire truth were permitted me."

In 1493, a woman named Caterina was living with Leonardo. This may have been his mother, as his letters suggest he invited her to live with him and she did not work as a servant. Caterina died a few years later, but the funeral was quite modest. Leonardo may not have wished to draw attention to his own humble and illegitimate origins.

Leonardo began work on the greatest art of his early career in 1495, The Last Supper, which was commissioned by Sforza for the refectory or dining hall of Santa Maria della Grazie in Milan. Sforza dined there twice each week and wanted an appropriate holy scene to gaze upon during his meals.

While depictions of the Last Supper vary and are typically relatively simple compositions showing Jesus and his disciples sharing a meal, Leonardo opted to portray the moment of the greatest drama, when Jesus announces that he will be betrayed. Leonardo grouped the disciples into gatherings of three, incorporating Judas with the other apostles, rather than placing him somewhat separately on the opposite side of the table. He focused on the drama of the moment and psychology of the apostles' facial expressions, choosing to isolate Judas not physically but by having him look away from Jesus and sitting in shadow. Making the painting even more unusual, Leonardo searched Milan to find models for both Christ and Judas. The use of models for a religious composition was distinctly unusual, but it is found throughout Leonardo's work.

Leonardo wrote in his notebooks, "A picture or representation of human figures, ought to be done in such a way as that the spectator may easily recognize, by means of their attitudes, the purpose in their minds." However, one of the lasting legacies of Leonardo's most famous works is that viewers often have a hard time deciphering what his subjects are thinking, a characteristic that has only added to the intrigue and mystique of works like Mona Lisa. Similarly, scholars have long disputed the iconography or symbolism of Leonardo's Last Supper, and some have gone so far as to suggest that the painting includes figures not typically found in depictions of the Last Supper, including Mary Magdalene. While many of these theories and accounts are not based in fact, Leonardo certainly thought carefully about each aspect of his composition, from the food on the table to the position of each apostle.

While Leonardo was a very skilled painter, he lacked a good technical understanding of fresco or perhaps was simply unwilling to alter his technique to accommodate the different medium. Frescoes were typically sketched out and worked in small sections. Water-based paint was applied to wet plaster, and as the plaster dried, the paint and plaster bonded, forming a long-lasting surface that tolerated dampness and variation in the wall surface due to climate changes. Adding depth and shading to a fresco requires great skill, particularly since the painting must be complete before the wet plaster dries each day.

   Rather than working with proper fresco technique, Leonardo attempted to layer paint on a dry gesso surface, working slowly and carefully, much as he would when working in oil or tempera on a wood panel or canvas. The paint did not adhere well to the dry plaster, and Leonardo often worked for a single long day and then stayed away for several days at a time, working on his own projects, studies and experiments. Thus, The Last Supper began to chip, flake and deteriorate as early as the beginning of the 16th century, within years of its completion in 1499.

   By the time the art historian Vasari visited Santa Maria della Grazie, the painting was already in very poor condition. The humidity in the refectory accelerated the damage; however, the space has been used as a stable and was nearly destroyed during bombing attacks in World War II. Only a recent restoration has improved the appearance of the Last Supper and preserved it from further damage. The heavily restored painting was cleaned and repaired, as needed, with the restorers relying on both extant paint and copies.

   Despite these efforts, however, the damage done to the painting over time has obscured the true appearance of Leonardo's composition as it was originally painted. Only a very small amount of Leonardo's original paint remains.

   While Leonardo worked on these paintings and compositions, he continued his personal studies and recorded them in his notebooks, typically maintaining four notebooks each devoted to a separate subject. The oldest of the notebooks extant today date to 1489, but his studies and research substantially predate these notebooks, and it is likely that he began keeping notebooks as early as the 1470s, during his apprenticeship to Verrocchio. Today, approximately 5000 pages of Leonardo's notebooks remain, all written in right-to-left mirror writing, meaning his notebooks were only legible when reflected in a mirror. He may have chosen mirror writing as a privacy measure or perhaps simply for speed, given that he was left-handed.

   As he filled each notebook, he eventually had them bound into larger volumes. It is through these notebooks, which covered architecture, painting, anatomy, optics, mechanics, and mathematics, that Leonardo's true genius becomes obvious.

   Leonardo made the acquaintance of many of the best minds of his time, including Fazio Cardan and Luca Pacioli. In 1498, Pacioli suggested the existence of a book on "Painting and Human Motion" by Leonardo and may have collaborated with Leonardo on a text on mathematics. Leonardo never perfected Latin or Greek, but he maintained long lists of Italian words and synonyms, ever desiring to improve his knowledge and skills. While Leonardo happily learned from others, he remained private about the details of many of his own designs, even in his notebooks.

   The work in these notebooks would have been revolutionary even in the 19th century.

Leonardo devised flying machines by studying and carefully recording information about birds and their wings, over 400 years before the Wright Brothers flew. He explored architectural design, ranging from churches and canals to great military fortresses, and his mechanical studies included work on hydraulics and engineering that led to a significant understanding of the movement of water and water currents. While his notebooks contained many of his designs, he also produced mechanical, architectural and engineering designs for patrons, including Sforza. In the course of his mechanical studies, he realized the fundamental nature of motion, foreshadowing Newton's work by more than two centuries. He also explained, in surprisingly accurate terms, the nature of light and light waves.

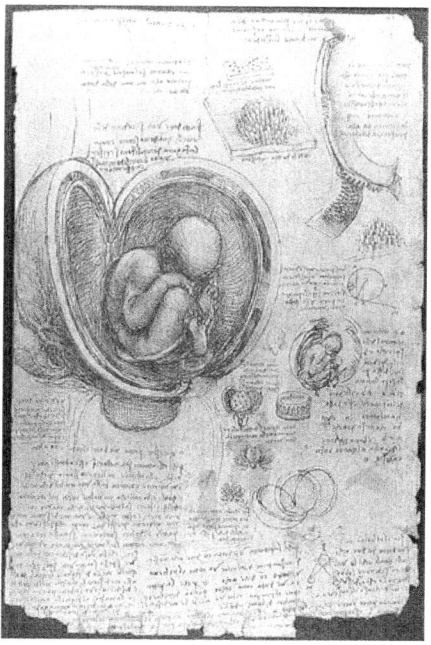

A page from Leonardo's Notebooks depicting a fetus in the womb

Leonardo observed people and took a particular interest in those he found unusual. His sketches and notes on human deformity began during his time in Florence, and he recorded notes on human anatomy following dissections, drawing sections of the muscles and organs. While dissection was not popular during this period, it was legal in limited circumstances and encouraged by Verrocchio. The conditions for dissections, called "anatomies" were deplorable and there was no means of preserving the corpse for study. Leonardo likely attended anatomies in Florence, Milan and Pavia. Some of his most intense work on anatomy took place around

1506 and 1507. His cross sections and careful drawings of various parts of the body date to this period. In Pavia, he also had the opportunity to explore optics and engage in scientific experimentation. He intended to create a book on human anatomy and may have been the first to draw not only the muscles, but the internal organs. Characteristically, Leonardo never completed this book.

Of all the work in the Notebooks, perhaps the most famous is the Vitruvian Man. What makes the drawing so remarkable is that it shows a male figure in two superimposed positions with his arms and legs apart, with both of the positions neatly fitted inside a circle and square. The artistic ability alone is impressive, but Leonardo used the circle and square to properly demonstrate the proportions of the human body, and for that reason the drawing and accompanying text are sometimes referred to as the Canon of Proportions or Proportions of Man.

The Vitruvian Man gets its name from the architect Vitruvius, and it is through the writings of Vitruvius that it becomes clear what Leonardo accomplished.

"For the human body is so designed by nature that the face, from the chin to the top of the forehead and the lowest roots of the hair, is a tenth part of the whole height; the open hand from the wrist to the tip of the middle finger is just the same; the head from the chin to the crown is an eighth, and with the neck and shoulder from the top of the breast to the lowest roots of the hair is a sixth; from the middle of the breast to the summit of the crown is a fourth. If we take the height of the face itself, the distance from the bottom of the chin to the under side of the nostrils is one third of it; the nose from the under side of the nostrils to a line between the eyebrows is the same; from there to the lowest roots of the hair is also a third, comprising the forehead. The length of the foot is one sixth of the height of the body; of the forearm, one fourth; and the breadth of the breast is also one fourth. The other members, too, have their own symmetrical proportions, and it was by employing them that the famous painters and sculptors of antiquity attained to great and endless renown. Similarly, in the members of a temple there ought to be the greatest harmony in the symmetrical relations of the different parts to the general magnitude of the whole. Then again, in the human body the central point is naturally the navel. For if a man be placed flat on his back, with his hands and feet extended, and a pair of compasses centred at his navel, the fingers and toes of his two hands and feet will touch the circumference of a circle described therefrom. And just as the human body yields a circular outline, so too a square figure may be found from it. For if we The Vitruvian Man gets its name from the architect Vitruvius, and it is through the writings of Vitruvius that it becomes clear what Leonardo accomplished. "For the human body is so designed by nature that the face, from the chin to the top of the forehead and the lowest roots of the hair, is a tenth part of the whole height; the open hand from the wrist to the tip of the middle finger is just the same; the head from the chin to the crown is an eighth, and with the neck and shoulder from the top of the breast to the lowest roots of the hair is a sixth; from the middle of the breast to the summit of the crown is a fourth. If we take the height of the face itself, the distance from the bottom of the chin to the under side of the nostrils is one third of it; the nose from the under side of the nostrils to a line between the eyebrows is the same; from there to the lowest roots of the hair is also a third, comprising the forehead. The length of the foot is one sixth of the height of the body; of the forearm, one fourth; and the breadth of the breast is also one fourth. The other members, too, have their own symmetrical proportions, and it was by employing them that the famous painters and sculptors of antiquity attained to great and endless renown. Similarly, in the members of a temple there ought to be the greatest harmony in the symmetrical relations of the different parts to the general magnitude of the whole. Then again, in the human body the central point is naturally the navel. For if a man be placed flat on his back, with his hands and feet extended, and a pair of compasses centred at his navel, the fingers and toes of his two hands and feet will touch the circumference of a circle described therefrom. And just as the human body yields a circular outline, so too a square figure may be found from it. For if we measure the distance from the soles of the feet to the top of the head, and then apply that measure to the outstretched arms, the breadth will be found to be the same as the height, as in the case of plane surfaces which are perfectly square."

The Vitruvian Man

Leonardo did not just dissect the bodies of people and animals; he also explored the world around him. During his explorations of the Italian countryside as a young man, Leonardo found and explored a cave. In this cave, he discovered a fossil fish and began to realize that the earth and creatures on the earth were far older than the Bible and Church had led him to believe. He privately rejected the notion of a Biblical flood, but he was not public about this realization. Refusing to take on the Church directly, Leonardo showed tact similar to the kind Copernicus employed a few generations later, and the kind Galileo eschewed to his own detriment.

While many of Leonardo's studies were academic and observational in nature, he also recorded his own philosophical thoughts in his many notebooks, filling each page with drawings and writings. His interest in philosophy extended to the psychology of painting. Such philosophical thinking is on display through his writings. "That is not riches, which may be lost; virtue is our true good and the true reward of its possessor. That cannot be lost; that never deserts us, but when life leaves us. As to property and external riches, hold them with trembling; they often leave their possessor in contempt, and mocked at for having lost them."

Politically, Sforza played Rome and France against one another and allied Milan with Venice,

Rome and Ferdinand of Aragon, King of Sicily and Spain in the League of Venice. The League of Venice was designed to oppose the French, and it forced Charles to retreat in 1495, but he returned a few years later. While his machinations worked for a time, even leading to a number of years of peace during the 1480s and 1490s, eventually, his plans failed. The French invaded Milan in 1499 and Ludovico Sforza was defeated. He regained control of Milan briefly, but the French were ultimately victorious, and with that Sforza was imprisoned and died in a French prison. Without Sforza's patronage, Leonardo needed to leave Milan and find a new patron and home.

Chapter 4: Florence

"It vexes me greatly that having to earn my living has forced me to interrupt the work and to attend to small matters." – The Notebooks of Leonardo

Leonardo spent at least some portion of later 1499 and early 1500, following the fall of Milan to the French, wandering. He visited Manua and drew a portrait of Isabella d'Este, but like many of Leonardo's other works, this portrait was not complete, forcing Isabella d'Este to write to Leonardo repeatedly over the coming years asking after the portrait. In Venice, Leonardo offered his services to the ruling council, including the designs for an underwater diving apparatus.

Leonardo's work on a portrait of Isabella d'Este, now in the Louvre

On April 24, 1500, Leonardo withdrew 600 florins from a Florentine bank and sent the money, along with a letter, to Florence before leaving Milan. Thus, it is likely that this date marks his return to the city of Florence. While Leonardo had left Florence while it was still under Medici rule, the Medici family had since been exiled and Florence had been occupied by the French, much like Milan. By 1500, the powerful Florentine merchant class had bought and bribed their way out of French control and the city was functioning as a republic, but serious military threats, including the papacy, the city of Pisa, the French and the remaining Medici family, remained. During these years, a religious sect led by Girolamo Savonarola gained power. While Savonarola himself was burned at the stake in 1498, his followers retained a significant amount of influence in the city.

Leonardo was no longer young, particularly by the standards of the early 16th century, but he was still quite healthy, energetic and vigorous, and some of his works, including the incomplete horse sculpture and The Last Supper, had made him famous across Italy. He was also respected for his scholarly work, particularly his studies of mathematics and science. At the same time, Florence was already home to an up-and-coming young artist, Michelangelo Buonarroti, and the young Michelangelo did not appreciate the arrival of Leonardo to the city. The two would soon become artistic rivals.

After his return, Leonardo paid a visit to his father, still living in the city with his fourth wife, and he took lodgings with the Servite friars and began work on an altarpiece featuring the Virgin Mary and her mother, St. Anne. Apocryphal tales about Anne were quite popular in Renaissance Italy. The cartoons and unfinished painting started in 1500 still exist, showing Mary with her child and St. Anne, looking quite serious.

Leonardo remained in Florence through 1501, working on smaller commissions. He travelled during 1502, designing a navigable canal for Cesare Borgia and spending time in both Mantua and Venice. He accompanied Borgia for a time, serving as his chief military engineer, and it was during this time that he also met Niccolo Machiavelli. He spent that winter in Imola with Borgia and drew the first known map to use a direct, overhead angle, but he left Borgia's employ in 1503 for reasons that remain unknown.

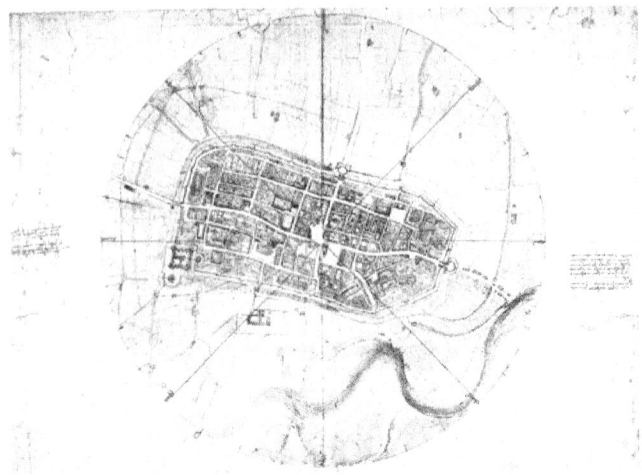

Leonardo's overhead view of Imola

Leonardo continued to work in the field of military engineering after his return to Florence. Machiavelli was working on plans to reroute the river, depriving Pisa of fresh water supplies, so Leonardo drew up a number of sketches and plans to alter the course of the river. The project, intended to secure a military victory in the war between Pisa and Florence, was never fully implemented. A labor force did begin digging a channel, but it was too shallow and ineffective. As an attempt would have been disastrous, the failure of this project was beneficial to both cities, but in the attempt Leonardo may have broadened Machiavelli's understanding of military and civil engineering.

During this time, Leonardo also began work on another large-scale fresco project, the Battle of Anghiari, on one wall of the Palazzo della Signoria or ruling council hall. But he was not the only painter hired to work on the paintings in the Palazzo della Signoria; a much younger Michelangelo was commissioned to paint a large battle scene, the Battle of Cascina, on the same wall in the council hall. Leonardo attempted to work with oil paints on dry plaster, this time adding wax to the linseed oil, but the paint began to separate from the plaster wall underneath from the beginning. Leonardo's weaknesses with fresco technique again led to failure and the painting began to deteriorate immediately. A few sketches exist, revealing a dark and tragic portrayal of war. A somewhat later copy by Peter Paul Rubens may illustrate some aspects of Leonardo's work, but it is very much in Rubens' style. By 1505, Leonardo had abandoned the project entirely, but at least he had completed the central portion of the scene before stopping work.

Rubens' depiction of Leonardo's work

Michelangelo did not complete his work either and may have barely moved past the initial drawings, but both the artists and the general public viewed these side-by-side paintings as a sort of contest or competition. Notably, while Michelangelo, now in his 30s, had finished many of his works prior to the work on the Palazzo della Signoria, he began to leave many works unfinished after this commission. In the 1560s, Giorgio Vasari, who wrote so much about both artists, was commissioned to paint over both Michelangelo and Leonardo's unfinished works in the Palazzo della Signoria, called the Palazzo Vecchio today.

Leonardo's interest in engineering and mechanics continued during this time, and he likely attempted to invent a flying machine during his years in Florence. He may also have made a preliminary attempt during his years in Milan. Based on the design in his notebooks, which was clearly based on the mechanics of a bird's wing, Leonardo would have been attempting to create a glider of sorts.

In 1504, the Florentine government called on Leonardo to design and supervise military fortifications at Piombino, revealing their ongoing respect for his broad skill set. The Renaissance fort is significantly different than its medieval predecessor. The French had entered Spain with large artillery, including cannons. While the medieval fortress was designed to stand up to siege warfare and armed troop assaults, the Renaissance fortress was built much more like a modern military bunker. It was low, impenetrable and could stand up to massive cannon fire. Angled walls helped to reduce the impact of artillery. Michelangelo would also go on to design similar fortifications during his career.

One of Leonardo's last projects, designed and constructed for the peace talks between the Pope and France, was a large Florentine lion. The mechanical lion took a few steps before a panel opened in its chest, revealing a French fleur-de-lys, the symbol of the French monarchy. While descriptions of the lion exist, Leonardo did not leave any sketches. The new French king, Francis I, was quite powerful, and the Medici family was eager to secure a peace treaty. Modern scholars have reconstructed the lion, which glides on its paws, swishes its tail, turns its head and opens its mouth in a silent roar.

Around early 1503, Leonardo began work in earnest on his most famous painting and one of the most famous paintings in history, the Mona Lisa. The Mona Lisa is likely a portrait of Lisa di Anto Maria di Noldo Gherardini, who had married Francesco di Bartolommeo de Zenobi del Giocondo in 1495. From her husband's name, Giocondo, she, and later her well-known portrait, gained the nickname La Joconde. The portrait may have been started as early as 1501, prior to Leonardo's work with Borgia or as late as 1505. While the portrait's subject was in all probability a Florentine noble woman, she never received the painting.

The Mona Lisa shows the serene woman in front of a rather harsh landscape, but in contrast to the landscape behind her, her face is quite delicate. While the painting has been poorly restored several times over the centuries, it likely was even finer than it appears today. Musicians entertained her while she sat for the portrait, providing the well-known Mona Lisa "smile". Soft shadows enhance the delicate tones of her skin.

The artistry of the Mona Lisa is impressive, but its unusual features have helped it endure as one of the most intriguing works of art in history. For that reason, there has long been speculation and rumor over just about every aspect of the Mona Lisa. While most believe the Mona Lisa is Lisa del Giocondo, a lack of definitive proof has long led others to speculate that Mona Lisa was Leonardo's mother Caterina drawn from memory, or even a self-portrait of Leonardo himself. Other aspects of the painting have long been questioned, including whether the surviving work is the original, and why Leonardo made it. The landscape in back of the Mona Lisa was also a novel effect, leading others to wonder how and why Leonardo drew it like that.

Of course, the most interesting aspect of the painting is the facial expression of the Mona Lisa, and for centuries people have argued over how Leonardo accomplished her enigmatic smile, or if it's even a smile at all. It is perhaps the most heavily analyzed aspect of any art in history, to an almost ridiculous extent. For example, scientific experiments about human vision have been used to explain why people characterize the nature of the smile differently, while one Harvard Professor has asserted that the nature of the smile changes based on whether a viewer looks at Mona Lisa's eyes or looks at the painting from a distance.

Years after making the Mona Lisa, Leonardo carried the painting with him to France, bequeathing it to Salai upon his death. Eventually it was purchased by King Francis I and remained in the possession of the French royal family until the French Revolution. Following the Revolution, the Louvre was opened to the public as an art museum, and it has housed Leonardo's Mona Lisa ever since.

Chapter 5: Final Years

"As a well-spent day brings happy sleep, so life well used brings happy death." – The Notebooks of Leonardo

In 1506, the French governor of Milan, Charles d'Amboise, summoned Leonardo to Milan. While the officials of the Florentine Republic repeatedly requested Leonardo's return, he opted to stay in Milan. His stay in Milan was quite short, but he worked on a second version of the Virgin of the Rocks during this time.

Shortly thereafter, he became the court artist and engineer for Louis XIII, King of France. He returned to Florence for approximately six months in 1507, in an attempt to secure a portion of his family inheritance after his father had died in 1504 without a will, but his legitimate brothers claimed the entire estate. Leonardo's uncle died in 1507, leaving him a generous inheritance, but his brothers attempted to claim that as well. Finally, Louis XIII wrote letters to the Florentine

Republic on Leonardo's behalf that helped him successfully inherit both money and land.

In 1513, Leonardo went to Rome, supported by the patronage of Giuliano de' Medici, the brother of Pope Leo X. Like the Medici family of the 15th century, this new generation continued to fund the work of Florentine artists, and by the second decade of the 16th century, a younger generation of artists was already working in Rome, including Michelangelo and Raphael. While Leonardo was still quite well-respected, these artists had secured many of the best commissions available in the city and the patronage of Pope Leo X. However, Leonardo did not come to Rome and the Vatican to paint; instead, he provided Guiliano de Medici with valuable engineering and military expertise. Pope Leo X was the son of Lorenzo de Medici, but he was not, by anyone's definition, a particularly holy man, and Giuliano served as the head of the papal army.

Pope Leo X

Over the next few years, Leonardo consulted on a number of private architectural and engineering projects, and though he was now approximately 60 years old, he remained active and relatively fit. He also continued his studies and experimentations during this period, designing the first solar panel, which he called a burning mirror. He also made a plan to drain the Pontine marsh, but it was not executed. An anecdotal story tells of Leonardo attaching wings to a lizard during this period.

While Leonardo continued to work on his notebooks, he was not allowed to participate in dissections and anatomies, and when he began to conduct some alchemical experiments, it likely displeased the Pope. Around 1510, he drew a rare self-portrait in his notebooks, again relying upon mirrors. The famous self-portrait in red chalk was drawn circa 1512-1515. Only one artistic commission can be attributed to this period, Leonardo's St. John the Baptist, one of the least-known and favored of Leonardo's works.

Around 1514, Leonardo began to experience weakness on the right side of his body. While this does not appear to have impacted his speech, it did reduce his ability to paint. Leonardo is believed to have been left-handed, so he was able to continue to write and sketch, but it no doubt reminded him of his mortality. He may have suffered a stroke during 1514 or perhaps had suffered another type of partial paralysis.

Leonardo joined the papal delegates at the 1515 peace talks in Bologna, presenting King Francis I with a mechanical lion. He was chosen as part of the delegation not because of his closeness to the Pope, but because of his past relationship and positive involvement with the French. While he worked closely with Giuliano de Medici, Leonardo was not close to Leo X and was subject to a variety of accusations, including necromancy. The notebooks from this period reveal an interest in alchemy, but Leonardo denounced necromancy in harsh and clear terms. Leonardo remained in Rome until 1516, when Giuliano died.

By 1516, younger artists had secured the patronage of powerful Italians, and the aging Leonardo again looked toward French patrons. After Giuliano's death in 1516, Leonardo finally accepted the offer of the French royal family, now led by King Francis I, to move to France. He made the long journey, accompanied by a single servant and the two men who had been part of his household since they were boys. Salai joined Leonardo's house in Milan, while Francesco

Melzi entered the makeshift family in 1506. As noted earlier, Leonardo's relationship with these young men is unclear. Salai does not appear to have been much of an artist, but a number of works have been attributed to Melzi, and some works attributed to Leonardo and his workshop as late as the 19th century have been re-attributed to Melzi recently. Leonardo took all of his possessions, including his paintings, notebooks and experiments with him on the long trip to Cloux, France. Leonardo was so well-respected and favored that the chateaux given to him by the French had a tunnel connecting his place to the royal family's own accommodations. For the rest of his years, Leonardo was treated with great respect by the French court and favored for his brilliant conversation.

The rich patronage of the French royal family provided Leonardo with the funds to devote himself largely to his scientific pursuits, and he produced relatively little art during these years. Instead, Leonardo conducted a number of physical experiments, including work with mechanics, hydraulics and optics. He may have completed a few works during these years, including St. John the Baptist, the Mona Lisa, and the Virgin and St. Anne, depending upon the state of his arm. Leonardo clearly made plans to publish his notebooks, organizing titles and chapter headings, but no further work was done on the publications of his work and it would fall upon others to publish them. His work was certainly hampered by the weakness on the right side of his body. By the time of his death, Leonardo's right arm was fully paralyzed.

In April 1519, Leonardo composed his will. He provided for Salai and his servant, leaving each of them a portion of the vineyard Sforza had given him as payment in 1499. Salai was also given the house in which he lived. Interestingly, Leonardo returned family property, including the inheritance he had fought for in Florence in 1507, to his brothers, along with a sum of cash. Melzi inherited the majority of Leonardo's estate and spent the remainder of his life carefully administering the legacy, and Melzi's descendants inherited Leonardo's notebooks. By 1630, the notebooks were in the possession of a Spanish sculptor who rebound the notebooks into a number of codices. Melzi returned to Italy, married and had a son after Leonardo died. He continued painting and his Flora now hangs in the Hermitage Museum.

Leonardo requested a lavish funeral, reflecting the young man who had planned great civic festivals and enjoyed the best things in life. Leonardo died on May 2, 1519. According to Vasari, Leonardo had reconciled himself with the Church by the end. Throughout Leonardo's work and notebooks, there is little mention of his personal faith; however, he apparently did make a final confession and take the sacraments before he died. Vasari recounts the death, stating that Leonardo died in the French King's arms; however, there is no other account of this.

The Clos Lucé, Leonardo's house and place of death in France

Chapter 6: Leonardo's Legacy

"What is fair in men, passes away, but not so in art." – The Notebooks of Leonardo

Painting Technique

While Leonardo completed relatively few works in comparison to some of his contemporaries, his skill is unquestioned, and the richness, color and depth of Leonardo's works can be attributed to a number of factors. While most Italian painters before Leonardo worked primarily in egg tempera paint, Leonardo favored oils. Egg tempera paints produce a relatively flat image, and the paint cannot be layered extensively and dries rather quickly, limiting the available work time. Tempera was most often painted on wooden panels. Oil painting developed in the North, particularly Flanders, and oil paints allowed for much greater depth, richer color, and a longer working time.

Leonardo's works began with sketches or cartoons, which could be quite small or full size, but either way they often laid out the composition and design of the finished work. Sketches were also used to work out details in paintings. The cartoons were typically drawn in charcoal and chalk, but some may have used a brown ink wash as well. Cartoons could be shown to a patron to approve a commission prior to beginning work on the actual painting.

Once the cartoons were complete, the design was transferred to the prepared canvas. Cartoons could be transferred to canvas in one of two ways. Many times the sketch was used as a sort of stencil. Holes were punched along the lines of the sketch and a bag of carbon dust pounced over the holes. The cartoon could also be used much like carbon paper. The back would be coated in carbon dust and the image traced. Surviving renaissance cartoons, including those by Leonardo, were typically unused. A remarkable cartoon of the Virgin and St. Anne survives, but differs from the painting of the same name.

Working on canvas, as he appeared to prefer, Leonardo painted the canvas with a layer of underpainting. The underpainting was light brown or gray in color, but provided the basis for the painting, including detailing areas of light and shadow. Leonardo produced a monochrome version of the finished painting as underpainting. Working with just a tone or two enabled the artist to easily correct areas that were too light or too dark. Later Flemish artists, including Peter Paul Rubens and Jan Vermeer, adopted simplified versions of Leonardo's painting technique. The underpainting is visible on the unfinished Adoration of the Magi.

While underpainting was not a new innovation in Leonardo's day, his avoidance of any sort of outline was. Even Leonardo's sketches and cartoons reveal a desire to avoid a strong outline, favoring soft shadows to distinguish shapes between the background and foreground. He replaced the traditional interiors used for portraits with detailed landscape backgrounds in a variety of works, including the Mona Lisa and Virgin of the Rocks.

With the underpainting in place, Leonardo began work on the painting. While oil painters often mix paint colors on a palette, Leonardo mixed his colors directly on the canvas. His works favor relatively muted tones, including shades of blue, green and brown. His paints were relatively transparent, but layered to provide a great deal of depth. These thin layers of paint enabled him to create the appearance of transparent fabrics and draperies. Darker tones provided the contrast between light and shadow, or chiaroscuro, which enabled Leonardo to model shapes, creating the impression of three dimensions. The use of transparent glazes, often tinted to a relatively dark shade is called sfumato, or "like smoke". The sfumato technique created the softness associated with Leonardo's work, particularly his portrayal of skin tones and faces, by blending the shadows and lights in the painting to create a smooth shift between tones. Leonardo also used velatura, a technique which changed the color or appearance of dry paint below it. A transparent glaze was rubbed into the surface of the painting, sometimes by hand. The glaze, typically quite thin, was both darker and warmer than the paint beneath it. While Leonardo used velatura, it is often more closely associated with the artwork of the Venetian renaissance.

The use of perspective was innovative in the Italian Renaissance. While earlier Renaissance artists had begun to use perspective, Leonardo developed and mastered vanishing point perspective, enabling him to create deep, three-dimensional compositions. The Virgin of the Rocks illustrates his use of perspective, particularly in the deep landscape background, while the unusual perspective of the The Last Supper enables Leonardo to illustrate the table, apostles and Christ in a single, flat composition, with Christ at its center.

Leonardo also played with perspective and optical illusions. The Mona Lisa's eyes appear to follow the viewer, creating a remarkably intriguing image that has held the attention of viewers for centuries.

Leonardo's Machines

While only a few of Leonardo's paintings survive, a much larger number of sketches for inventions, engineering projects and machines have been preserved, many of which were found in his notebooks. Leonardo did build small models of some of his projects, but these do not survive. It is unknown how many of his designs were constructed or attempted during his lifetime, but he does mention some attempts.

In January 1496, Leonardo wrote of his intention to try one of his flying machines. While nobody knows the results of his test, Leonardo noted that further flying attempts should take place over a lake to reduce the risk of injury. Later parachute designs may have been intended for pilot safety. Modern reconstructions have revealed that Leonardo's designs could very well have worked as he intended if properly constructed.

A number of working reconstructions of Leonardo's designs have been built by modern engineers, including a mechanical weaving loom and a diving suit. Leonardo's loom was not, as far as modern scholars know, ever built, but his design included the first horizontal view of a loom. He automated the functions then performed by a weaver by hand. The reconstruction used aspects of four different loom designs by Leonardo.

Leonardo's interest in water led to at least two diving suit designs. One of these diving suits, consisting of a helmet with a breathing tube connected to a cork and wood float, was built by the British Broadcasting Corporation and found to be an effective option, comparable to early diving suits of a much later period, after a modern diver tested the suit in shallow waters. A second design included a wineskin to hold air, as well as a pouch for urine to allow the diver to remain underwater for a longer time. While this design has never been built, similar designs were used for the first effective diving suits.

In 1502, Leonardo designed a single span bridge, intended to span the inlet of the Golden Horn in Turkey, but the bridge design was not considered feasible and was refused. A smaller version was built in Norway in 2001 and work began on Leonardo's design, worked in full, in its intended location on the Golden Horn in 2006. While the single span bridge was intended to be a permanent installation, Leonardo also designed a portable bridge intended for military use. The revolving bridge could be placed on one side of a river and swung into place with a rope-and-pulley system. A counterweight on the opposite side helped to secure it. The bridge, designed to be pulled by a team of horses, enabled troops and horses to cross water with ease. Other bridges designed for military use included a quick-construction bridge that could be assembled and disassembled for use by the military.

Other reconstruction attempts include Leonardo's 70-foot crossbow, a flying glider and a parachute. These reconstructions provided the basis for a Public Broadcasting System documentary on Leonardo's inventions. Leonardo's parachute was effective and provided a smooth ride; however, it was quite heavy and posed a risk to the skydiver upon landing. Leonardo's design was hand-held, without a harness. The modern parachute, folded and launched via a ripcord, was not invented until 1920.

Leonardo's glider was flown by a skilled hang glider, but it required the addition of a tail for stability. His other designs for flying machines relied upon a flapping motion, like a bird's wing.

Leonardo's crossbow, designed to be mounted on wheels, was made of lightweight wood for flexibility. The crossbow was not designed to shoot arrows, but was likely intended to shoot barrels or some sort of flaming projectile. Though he later characterized war as "bestial" and seemed to have a strong distaste for it, Leonardo's crossbow illustrates his understanding of the importance of visual impact and morale in warfare. The giant weapon would have, without a doubt, been a horrifying sight for opponents.

A 1588 English translation of Italian military works mentions Leonardo's close association with the military engineer Francesco di Giorgio and describes weapons that may have been based on Leonardo's designs. The English employed a number of new devices and technologies in their battle against the Spanish Armada in 1588, many of which bear a distinct resemblance to Leonardo's designs. Leonardo's sketches may have contributed to multi-barreled guns and incendiary weapons built and used against the Spanish.

The Vitruvian Man

While Leonardo's paintings are among the most recognized in the world, one of his sketches is also particularly well-known. The Vitruvian Man depicts a nude male figure with limbs outstretched. The design is based on the principles of Vitruvius, the first century Roman architect. The figure is surrounded by both a square and circle, with limbs moving to accommodate the outlined shape. Text surrounding the figure explains the idea of perfect proportion and symmetry. According to Vitruvius, the proportions of the human body were the ideal model for the proportions of architecture. During the classical revival of the Italian renaissance, the work of Vitruvius was rediscovered and newly appreciated.

The Vitruvian Man is a study in proportion, helping the viewer to understand how various parts of the body relate to one another. While Leonardo's Vitruvian Man was not the first such image, his image does account for the change in the proportions of the figure as the body moves. Leonardo's Vitruvian Man has two sets of legs and two sets of arms, rather than just one. Lines on the form mark off portions of the body. Like other works by Leonardo, the figure appears to be modeled on a real person, complete with messy hair and distinct facial features, and some have speculated it was based on a cadaver.

While Leonardo had a strong understanding of proportion, he did not always choose to apply his understanding to his paintings. Works like The Last Supper reveal his willingness to alter proportion to achieve a desired effect. In the case of The Last Supper, Christ's hands are usually large, drawing attention to his hand position and movements. At times, the message or significance of the piece was more important than anatomical correctness or classically influenced proportion for Leonardo.

Vasari's Biography

Leonardo was a relatively private man. While he recorded a great deal about his observations and studies, he did so without revealing a lot of himself. But contemporary records do exist, and scholars also rely upon the work of the first art historian, Giorgio Vasari (1511-1577), who had access to materials that have now been lost and provided a rather thorough, but not entirely accurate, portrayal of the first true Renaissance man. He published the first version of the "Lives of the Most Excellent Painters, Sculptors and Architects" in 1550, less than 35 years after Leonardo's death. Vasari was certainly not objective and was very much enamored of Leonardo's work and intellect. He includes both rumors and legends and is often not accurate with attributions and dates.

Vasari begins with a discussion of the artist's childhood, talking about his quick mind and diverse interests even as a small boy. From Vasari, readers learn that Leonardo learned rapidly, challenging his instructors and that his father arranged his apprenticeship with Verrocchio. He provides details about Leonardo's apprenticeship, including mentioning a number of fine relief sculptures, now lost. He tells of cartoons for wall hangings and repeats a rumor supporting both Leonardo's interest in the natural world and his fine painting skill. According to Vasari, Ser Piero sent a buckler or shield made by a local countryman to Leonardo. Leonardo repaired the buckler, improving its appearance and quality and painted it with a monstrous scene of lizards, insects and bats. He used dead animals as models and worked seemingly unaware of the odor. The final creature was, according to Vasari, "most horrible and terrifying". Ser Piero purchased another buckler for the peasant and sold Leonardo's. While there is no corroborating evidence for Vasari's account, it does illustrate Leonardo's near-obsessive interest in nature. Vasari describes a number of paintings, works on paper and sculptures that have been lost over the years, often describing them in some detail.

While Vasari was particularly concerned with Leonardo's sculpture and painting, he also mentions his design and engineering skill and projects. He mentions Leonardo's architectural drawings, plans for water-driven flour mills, and efforts in hydraulic engineering. Vasari also mentions Leonardo's interest in both philosophy and alchemy.

Modern Science

Modern science may provide some previously unknown insights into Leonardo's life and work.

Advances in scientific technology, from fingerprinting to x-rays, offer new options for learning about the man and his art. Scientists and scholars have reconstructed Leonardo's fingerprint, using multiple partial prints from some 52 works attributed to Leonardo and have discovered lost works by the great artist. These technological leaps may help to identify unknown works or confirm others attributed to him.

Leonardo's fingerprints suggest that his mother might have been Arab by birth, perhaps originally from Turkey, as many slaves were brought into Northern Italy in the early Renaissance from the Ottoman Empire. Other theories about his mother's origins identify her as a Jew, perhaps originally from Russia. While fingerprints are far from a certain means of determining ethnicity, they may eventually provide insights into what Leonardo ate or where he travelled.

Fingerprint evidence may already have allowed art historians to positively identify at least one of Leonardo's lost works. A portrait of a young woman, previously considered to be of 19th century German origin, was the first major work of Leonardo's identified in more than a century. The pre-eminent Leonardo scholar, Martin Kemp, had already possibly attributed the painting to Leonardo on the basis of style and quality. Leonardo often used his fingers to apply glazes, blend colors or work the surface of pencil, chalk and charcoal drawings, and the fingerprint found in this piece, called La Bella Principessa, may have similarities to prints identified as belonging to Leonardo. Using fingerprints to identify and attribute paintings is relatively new technology and remains largely the work of a single forensic art historian, Peter Paul Biro. Biro's work has been controversial and there have been accusations of dishonesty. While La Bella Principessa may be a lost Leonardo, the evidence remains somewhat unclear.

La Bella Principessa

Science has also provided insights into other lost works by Leonardo. Modern technology is being used to investigate the wall in the Palazzo Vecchio on which Leonardo painted the Battle of Anghiari. Vasari's battle scene has long been believed to cover the lost work by Leonardo; however, the Leonardo was believed to have been destroyed by Vasari's work. In the 1970s, a scholar noted the words "cerca trova" on a flag in Vasari's painting. This phrase, which means "seek and you shall find" led to renewed interest in Leonardo's work and the suspicion that Vasari may have, in 1550, actually worked to preserve the great work. Microwave and ultraviolet testing has revealed a gap between Vasari's fresco and the surface beneath, suggesting that the artist may have intentionally spared whatever remained of Leonardo's composition. A small camera has been threaded through a hole bored into Vasari's painting, between the two surfaces, confirming the existence of a false wall and a hollow between the surfaces. Additional testing was planned, but only limited work has been allowed, largely on cracked or restored portions of the Vasari composition. Tests have also revealed black pigment in the hollow. While this may be the location of Leonardo's Battle of Anghiari, the evidence is not definitive and further testing will be required to confirm the possibility.

Leonardo's Influence

While Leonardo never ran a workshop and took on only two pupils, neither of whom was particularly talented, his work has had a lasting impact on the history of art, and he is widely recognized as one of the greatest artists of all time. From a solely artistic standpoint, Leonardo was less influential than some of his contemporaries, including Michelangelo, if only because he didn't take on apprentices. Artists who maintained workshops and took on apprentices often had a larger influence on the art that followed.

A Treatise on Painting, possibly compiled by Melzi, was published after Leonardo's death. The Treatise on Painting includes excerpts and pages from Leonardo's notebooks on painting and provides a great deal of information about his philosophy of painting. During his lifetime, Leonardo's works were well-known, both in the original form and copies and prints. Contemporaries certainly visited, studied and copied his works, particularly those on public display.

His influence is seen in the use of chiaroscuro, sfumato, and perspective in the artwork of the artists of the late Italian Renaissance, including Corregio, Raphael, and Del Sarto. The drama of Leonardo's compositions is echoed and expanded upon by later Baroque artists, like Caravaggio. Leonardo's mastery of oil painting influenced later Northern artists, including Peter Paul Rubens and Rembrandt van Rijn. An extant copy of the Battle of Anghiari by Rubens exists today.

Leonardo's research, engineering and design went largely unnoticed during his lifetime, and most of his inventions were never built or attempted for centuries. He may have had some influence on military design and weaponry, but he would never have been mistaken for Clausewitz either.

Ultimately, much of Leonardo's genius would come to the forefront centuries after he had lived, and even then it would require the actual construction of some of the objects he had envisioned to truly appreciate his revolutionary conceptions. Among other things, Leonardo envisioned a helicopter, a tank, a calculator, a double hulled ship, and even a rudimentary theory of plate tectonics. He also conceptualized an automated bobbin winder and a machine for testing the tensile strength of wire, which would be created long after his life. Had Leonardo's designs and works been widely disseminated and truly understood, there's no telling how much more technologically advanced the world could have been in the ensuing centuries.

While Leonardo was a visionary, his visions, theories and designs came before the world was ready to build or accept them.

Bibliography

Capra, Fritjof. The Science of Leonardo: Inside the Mind of the Great Genius of the Renaissance. New York, NY: Anchor Books, 2008.

Nuland, Sherwin B. Leonardo da Vinci. New York, NY: Penguin Books, 2005.

"Leonardo da Vinci". The Heilbrunn Timeline of Art History. http://www.nationalgallery.org.uk/artists/leonardo-da-vinci (accessed on July 21, 2012).

"Leonardo da Vinci". Medici: Godfathers of the Renaissance. http://www.pbs.org/empires/medici/renaissance/leonardo.html (accessed on July 21, 2012).

"Leonardo da Vinci". The National Gallery. http://www.nationalgallery.org.uk/artists/leonardo-da-vinci (accessed on July 21, 2012).

Michelangelo

Chapter 1: Family Life, Florence, and Foster Care

Michelangelo Buonarroti was born on March 6, 1475 in Caprese, a small village near Tuscany, Italy that has since been renamed Caprese Michelangelo after its most famous resident. He was the second-oldest child born to Ludovico Buonarroti and Francesco Neri del Miniato di Siena.

Though Michelangelo was born in Caprese, his family was concentrated in Florence, and his family would move back to Florence shortly after his birth. The circumstances that brought the family to Caprese were unusual; the year before Michelangelo's birth, Ludovico had been appointed podesta of the Caprese and Chiusi villages. This anachronistic position involved relatively little work, and essentially consisted of presiding over the local court. He was endowed with the authority to convict and effect sentences, but in practice the job was hardly stressful.

The reasons for leaving Caprese reflect profound insecurity on the part of Ludovico, and his insecurities would hinder Michelangelo throughout his own life. Specifically, Caprese was a country village that paled in prestige to Florence, despite the fact that Florence itself had lost some luster over the preceding century, and Ludovico descended from a long lineage of wealthy Florentine bankers. It was difficult for him to accept the prospect of moving to a village that he would not have deigned moved to in earlier decades.

Although the anecdote has not been verified, Ludovico was fond of claiming that his family descended from Countess Mathilde di Canossa. However, in the decades preceding Michelangelo's birth, the family had fallen into a state of decadence, and Ludovico's grandfather squandered much of the family fortune. By the time Ludovico was born, the family had already lost much of their wealth and standing in Florence, but there was a stark contrast between the pride Ludovico held for his family name and his own lack of money. On the one hand, he was resolutely unwilling to accept employment as an artisan, but at the same time he possessed little money. Ultimately, George Bull summed up the living situation best when he wrote, "In early manhood Ludovico lived in genteel poverty, with an eye diffidently open for the main chance. He was set in the belief that people of good descent should be able to subsist on patronage or rents." Essentially, Ludovico was unwilling to work hard and felt that his family lineage should have precluded him from needing to secure gainful employment.

By the time Michelangelo was born, Ludovico was already 31 years of age. He was 11 years older than his wife, and by the standards of the time period, he had already reached a relatively advanced stage in life for someone who had never settled into a career. Although he was not fond of his position as podesta, the irony is that he would likely have been unable to even obtain the position were it not for his family pedigree. Ludovico's distaste for Caprese may seem excessive today, but in 15th century Italy, people were extraordinarily provincial, and Ludovico had plenty of reasons to be particularly proud of Florence. Still, in order to pay his expenses, Ludovico often resorted to pawning the family belongings, and the move to Caprese was borne out of sheer desperation.

Meanwhile, Michelangelo's mother Angela was significantly younger than her husband. They had married in 1472 and given birth to an older child the following year. Although her family did not possess the noble pedigree of her husband, Angela came from an artistic background, leading many to assume that Michelangelo inherited his artistic talents from her. Her family has also been credited with the invention of a red dye that was popularly used for painting, and her family associated with artistic luminaries of the early Renaissance like Leon Battista Alberti.

A statue of Alberti in Florence

Although it is uncertain what brought Ludovico and Angela together, especially given their discrepancy in age, they held a mutual distaste for Caprese and moved back to Florence the year after Michelangelo was born. Ludovico did not have any clear job opportunities while in Florence, yet he had inherited property in the Santa Croce region of the city, a decent plot of land that included a farm. Although Santa Croce was not the prestigious section of the city, moving away from Caprese brought considerable comfort to Ludovico. While in Florence, the family expanded to include three younger brothers, all born two years apart: Buonarotto in 1477, Giovansimone in 1479, and Gismondo in 1481. In retrospect, it is surprising that the family grew during this time period, particularly since Angela was constantly in poor health. Almost from the beginning, she was unfit to nurse Michelangelo, and he was effectively raised by a wet nurse throughout his infancy. At the same time, hiring a wet nurse would have been difficult for the financially strapped Ludovico, but being able to afford a wet nurse was a major status symbol in contemporary Florentine society, and it relieved Ludovico and his wife from the more unpleasant child-rearing tasks. While it is true that Angela was physically unable to nurse Michelangelo, the possibility remains that they would have hired a wet nurse even if Angela had been healthier.

The importance of the wet nurse has also been mythologized in the narrative of Michelangelo's life. The wet nurse was the daughter of a stonecutter, and her husband also served as one. As a result, later in life Michelangelo would state that he had been breast-fed on the milk of sculptors. In light of this dynamic, it is easy to reach the conclusion that Michelangelo was destined to become a sculptor almost from birth. Michelangelo's anecdote concerning breast-feeding also reveals how he conceived of his wet nurse as his mother and was closer to her than with Angela. In addition to not rearing him, Angela never offered him any warmth or affection either. After living for years with illness, she passed away in 1482, when Michelangelo was just 6 years old.

Although he had never been close to his mother, her death transformed the family dynamic and struck Michelangelo hard. Despite his young age, Michelangelo became increasingly sullen in demeanor. Making matters worse, Ludovico was tasked with raising five children, one of whom had been born just one year before, and his poor work ethic made this situation untenable. With no viable alternative, Ludovico sent Michelangelo to live with a foster family, where he was raised (ironically enough) by a stonecutter and his wife. With his foster family, he received a standard upbringing and played with his foster brothers and sisters. More importantly, however, it was while spending time with his surrogate father that he learned many of the marble-handling skills that he would later apply in his own career.

Despite sending his son to live with another family, Ludovico still held great ambition for his second-oldest son. He was a proud man and was ever-cognizant of the need to resurrect his family's standing. When Michelangelo was 10 years old, he was sent to the prestigious grammar school of Francesco da Urbino, where he was taught Latin but never applied himself enough to be a good student. As his later output of sonnets would attest, Michelangelo was far from unintelligent or incapable of grasping Latin; the teenager was simply unwilling to invest himself in his studies, particularly since he was becoming ever more interested in art.

Michelangelo's academic shortcomings distressed Ludovico, who was unenthusiastic about his son's interest in art. Always subsumed in matters of family status, Ludovico was deeply affected by the fact that artists were viewed analogously to artisans. They were not the public celebrities that they would later become, and even though the social climate was changing, Ludovico saw no difference between artists and laborers when it came to class prestige. Nevertheless, there was nothing he could do to transform his son, who had not lived with his father for roughly five years and was less and less inclined to please Ludovico.

While Ludovico had all sorts of qualms about Michelangelo's direction, it was clear from a young age that Michelangelo had a prodigious artistic talent. Making art was not a diversion for him but a chosen career course that he already mapped out from an early age. His studies were not neglected out of insolence but rather abandoned so that he had time to paint copies of churches.

Michelangelo's schooling did result in one fortuitous development. One of his classmates was Francesco Granacci, who would later become a famous artist in his own right. Granacci was also a student in the workshop of the decorated painter Dominco Ghirlandaio. Granacci and Michelangelo quickly became friends, and Granacci began bringing his younger friend with him for workshop sessions. When it became clear that Michelangelo would not advance in his academic studies, he gained admittance into Ghirlandaio's workshop after Ludovico begrudgingly acquiesced. In an unusual dynamic, Michelangelo's father was also able to secure a rare system in which his son was actually paid for his apprenticeship. According to the contemporary biographer Vasari, Ludovico wrote down the arrangement in a book:

> "1488. bow this 1st April that I Ludovico di Lionardo Buonarroto apprentice my son Michelangelo to Domenico and David di Tommaso di Currado for the next three years, with the following agreements: that the said Michelangelo shall remain, with them that time to learn to paint and practise that art and shall do what they bid him, and they shall give him 24 florins in the three years, 6 in the first, 8 in the second and 10 in the third, in all 96 lire…Michelangelo has received 2 gold florins this 16th April, and I Ludovico di Lionardo, his father, have received 12 lire 12 soldi."

This is believed to be a self-portrait of Dominco Ghirlandaio

Chapter 2: Artistic Education

> "As when, O lady mine,
> With chiselled touch
> The stone unhewn and cold
> Becomes a living mould,
> The more the marble wastes,
> The more the statue grows." – Michelangelo, Sonnet addressed to Vittoria Colonna

Michelangelo's admittance into the workshop was the most significant event in his life thus far. The education he received from Ghirlandaio would trump his formal academic education and give him the foundation needed to succeed as a professional artist. Beginning with his first day at the workshop on April 1, 1488, Michelangelo would permanently be recognized as an artist.

The system that Michelangelo entered into at the Ghirlandaio workshop was something of a hybrid between a vocational program and an academic art institution. Art was approached with rigorous discipline, and art students were expected to perfect a diverse variety of techniques across different media. At the same time, students were educated on the works of canonical artistic luminaries such as Giotto, Masaccio, and Santo Spirito. It's safe to assume that Michelangelo was already familiar with famous artists from previous time periods and their different artistic styles, but in this regard the workshop possessed an academic character. Students were expected to master drawing, incorporating techniques such as cross-hatching, a technique popularized by engravers such as Martin Schongauer.

An engraving of the Passion of Christ by Schongauer

It was immediately evident that Michelangelo was talented beyond his years, and for better or worse, he was well aware of his talents and considered himself to be artistically superior to his own instructor. In one instance, he took it upon himself to improve upon a work completed by Ghirandaio himself. Vasari described the anecdote:

"One of the youths happened one day to have made a pen sketch of draped women by his master, Michelangelo took the sheet, and with a thicker pen made a new outline for one of the women, representing her as she should be and making her perfect. The difference between the two styles is as marvellous as the audacity of the youth whose good judgment led him to correct his master. The sheet is now in my possession, treasured as a relic. I had it from Granaccio with others of Michelangelo, to place in the Book of Designs. In 1550, when Giorgio showed it to Michelangelo at Rome, he recognised it with pleasure, and modestly said that he knew more of that art when a child than later on in life.

One day, while Domenico was engaged upon the large chapel of S. Maria Novella, Michelangelo drew the scaffolding and all the materials with some of the apprentices at work. When Domenico returned and saw it, he said, 'He knows more than I do,' and remained amazed at the new style produced by the judgment of so young a boy, which was equal to that of an artist of many years' experience. To this Michelangelo added study and diligence so that he made progress daily"

Given Michelangelo's attitude and actions, it's not terribly surprising that he developed a reputation not only for his artistic skills but for his difficult personality as well. However, despite his ego, there was no denying his talent, as evidenced by one of his earliest paintings, which dates to 1487 or 1488, when Michelangelo was either 12 or 13 years old.

The Torment of Saint Anthony

   Entitled *The Torment of St. Anthony*, the work was painted using oil and tempera and inspired by Martin Schongauer's engraving, *The Temptation of St. Anthony* (1470s). It depicts the eponymous Saint while he is attacked in the desert by a collection of monsters. This subject matter was a popular one during the time period, and Schongauer's influence was widespread throughout the region. Still, there are esoteric aspects of the painting that are eclectic in their own right and shed light on Michelangelo's later career. First, the use of highly saturated colors is one of the most striking aspects of the work; the vivid colors and fantastical subject matter combine for an almost comic book-like quality. Throughout his career, Michelangelo continued to paint with such vibrancy and spatial confusion, a clear departure from the more naturalistic compositions that characterized the naturalism and geometric rigidity of the burgeoning Renaissance style. Another aspect of note is the scales on the backs of several of the monsters. In order to achieve such realistic scales, Michelangelo visited the fish market and studied the animals. As a result, he achieved particularly realistic scales, and the painting ultimately contains a complex balance between its fantastical subject matter and realistic motifs such as the scales.

Although Michelangelo had a difficult personality, Ghirlandaio was fully aware of his talent and understood that his star pupil would need to receive a more rigorous outlet in which to hone his craft. Fortunately for Michelangelo, Ghirlandaio had strong connections with the Medici family, the ruling family of Florence. In 1489, Lorenzo de' Medici asked Ghirlandaio for his two best pupils, as he had two openings for his Neo Platonic Humanist Academy. Michelangelo and his friend Granacci were the two selected, and they entered the Academy immediately following the decision.

Chapter 3: The Medici Art Academy and Medici Palace

It may seem strange that the ruler of Florence should be invested in art to the extent of operating an art academy, but Lorenzo de' Medici was one of the major proponents of the Humanist movement, a philosophical tradition of which Florence was an epicenter. The so-called Neoplatonists, including Marsilio Ficino, Pico della Mirandola, and Leonardo da Vinci, spread the Humanist principles of rational thought and worldly endeavor. Where art had previously been under the authority of the Church, by the late 15th century it became more widespread for art to be produced "for art's sake." Artistic connoisseurs and patrons became more commonplace, and Lorenzo de' Medici was chief among such patrons.

Michelangelo's time in the Medici Academy constituted a major period of growth for his artistic and intellectual development. While there, he became especially astute in sculpture, studying the art under the famous sculptor Bertoldo di Giovanni, and his studies also included reading texts by noted Humanist philosophers such as Marcilio Ficino and Pico della Mirandola. In addition to acquiring technical proficiency in different artistic media, reading significant philosophical texts enabled Michelangelo to understand and add a more scientific and theoretical dimension to his art.

Two events of particular significance took place while Michelangelo was at the Academy. First, in 1489, he met Lorenzo de' Medici in the garden of San Marco, which at the time was a center for intellectual engagement among artists. It was believed that by giving the students a shared place in which to work, they could benefit from their mutual interactions and achieve accelerated artistic growth. One day, Lorenzo visited the garden and noticed a sculpture

Michelangelo had completed of an old man, a lost sculpture now known as *Head of the Faun* (1489). Impressed by the work, Lorenzo initiated conversation, but he told Michelangelo, "You ought to know that the old never have all their teeth, and always lack some." noting that the sculpture would have been even more realistic if the man had fewer teeth." Immediately after this comment Michelangelo removed one of the teeth, which Lorenzo later took as a measure of respect and devotion. This episode led to Lorenzo inviting Michelangelo to stay with him in the nearby palace at Via L'Arga, where he was granted unprecedented privileges, afforded the privilege of an allowance (five ducats per day), a velvet cloak, and the right to sit with the family during meals. Living at the Medici palace represented a major status symbol, and it also supplied the young artist one of his most cherished patrons. Michelangelo enjoyed his time in the Medici Palace, and he would later refer to it as the happiest period of his life.

However, the second major event that took place during his studies at the Academy was an unfortunate one. In 1492, after three years of living in the Medici Palace, Michelangelo became involved in an intense conflict with a classmate named Pietro Torrigiano. The two were in the Church of the Carmine, a popular place for the students to draw, and Michelangelo made an arrogant remark. In response, Torrigiano struck Michelangelo on the nose, an injury for which he would bear the effects for the remainder of his life. Even in late portraits of Michelangelo, viewers can notice his flattened nose, which would come to represent one of his defining physical characteristics. The episode should not only be interpreted as the event that forever changed his facial appearance, but also for the way in which it sheds light on Michelangelo's personality; he was fully aware of his artistic talents and was often cruel or insensitive to his less-skilled classmates. Moreover, it was no doubt a point of irritation for his classmates that Michelangelo was afforded the singular privilege of being allowed to stay in the Medici Palace, and this fight reflected the tensions that existed between the young master and his classmates.

While at the Medici Academy, Michelangelo produced his first significant sculptures. The first of these was *Madonna of the Stairs*, which was made from marble and bears little similarity to *The Torment of St. Anthony*.

Madonna of the Stairs

    The eclectic shapes of his earlier painting are replaced with more rigidly-defined shapes, the monochromatic color scheme obviously constitutes a clear departure from the saturated colors of *The Torment of St. Anthony*, and the gold coloration recalls the dominant color tones of Byzantine art. Michelangelo would later come to resent this early work, disavowing the schiacciato, low-relief style that placed the figures in an almost two-dimensional position. Furthermore, he had borrowed the technique from Donatello, and he was embarrassed at having copied the signature of one of the leading sculptors. Ultimately, the sculpture is impressive in its own right, but its linearity remains out of place when compared with Michelangelo's later works.

    Although Michelangelo borrowed the techniques of other sculptors, the sculpture was unusual in a number of respects. While Michelangelo depicts a Madonna with Child composition, he resists certain tropes associated with the famous symbol. First, Mary does not gaze at her son; she appears distracted, as though something were taking place in the distance that required her to divert her attention away from the baby Jesus. Second, there are a series of figures in the background on the stairs. While most Madonna compositions are arrested in time, capturing the intimate moment between mother and child as though it transcended time, Michelangelo portrays the archetype as though it were a snapshot. In so doing, he adds a naturalistic dimension to the work that was more contemporary than the Byzantine coloration would initially suggest. Additionally, astute observers will notice that the lighting for the Baby Jesus is slightly brighter than the other figures, corresponding with the fact that he is situated closest to the fore. As such, Michelangelo borrows from the light gradations that were beginning to infiltrate contemporary art during the early Renaissance.

Another significant work completed during this period, and the last Michelangelo would finish while at the Medici Palace, was *Battle of the Centaurs* (1492).

Battle of the Centaurs

Although this composition was also made from marble and was completed just one year after *Madonna of the Stairs*, it is in many ways more similar to *The Torment of St. Anthony* than to the earlier sculpture. Specifically, the chaotic jumbling of shapes represented an unusual decision by early Renaissance standards. Where *Madonna of the Stairs* features an almost two-dimensional spatial calculus, in *Battle of the Centaurs* the figures are far more three-dimensional. The violent subject matter and entanglement of figures coheres more firmly with the style of his earlier painting than with his prior sculpture. The scene depicted refers to a battle between the Lapiths and the Centaurs.

On a formal level, the work is of great significance because it is the first example of Michelangelo's tendency to craft compositions that appear unfinished. At the top of the work, viewers can see the rough marks of the Subbia Chisel; in refraining from smoothening them out, Michelangelo makes the work appear far coarser than customary. In another rare move, he avoided using a bow drill, preferring instead to use a toothed chisel and gradina. As a result, the finished product has an unpolished yet ultimately more realistic appearance.

Chapter 4: On the Road

Unfortunately for Michelangelo, 1492 not only saw the nurturing of his artistic style but also great disappointment. Lorenzo de' Medici, Michelangelo's greatest proponent, passed away that year, forcing the young artist to leave the Medici court. By this time, his father had remarried, but Ludovico continued to suffer economic difficulties. In an effort to assist Ludovico, Michelangelo returned to Florence late in 1492, but it was not easy to find employment. After losing Lorenzo de' Medici, he needed to find a new patron.

Thankfully, the Church of Santa Maria del Santo Spirito commissioned him to complete a polychrome wood sculpture, which was simply titled *Crucifix* (1493).

Crucifix

Michelangelo rarely completed such overtly Biblical topics, and one might be tempted to overlook the work as simply being the product of the need to support his father. However, the production of *Crucifix* facilitated the development of his later style as well. In particular, he was given access to the corpses that emerged from the hospital at Santo Spirito, and Michelangelo completed rigorous diagrams of the bodies of the deceased. Like Leonardo, Michelangelo dissected the corpses, and while he did not enjoy the morbid activity, it was done in the spirit of achieving greater realism in his art. In *Crucifix*, it is readily apparent that Michelangelo was familiar with the wan appearance of the deceased body, and he portrays Christ with a realistic figure that was largely unprecedented during the time period. It is also notable that Christ does not even appear with a loincloth; throughout his career, Michelangelo would become famous for his liberal use of nudity, a trend that began with this work. Although male nudity was a dominant trope of ancient art, nudity is treated in more ideal, muscular terms throughout antiquity, whereas Michelangelo's treatment was far more realistic. Thus, despite agreeing to complete an iconic composition mainly out of financial necessity, Michelangelo added his personal signature to the work.

Michelangelo's stay back home would prove to be short-lived. In January of 1494, he was called upon by Pietro de' Medici, successor to Lorenzo, to complete a sculpture related to a recent snowstorm. This time, however, Michelangelo clashed with Pietro from the start, and while the artist had a difficult personality, in this case his dislike for Piero was understandable. The young Medici mismanaged the empire, and the Medici family was eventually expelled from Florence altogether. Aware that this development was about to take place, Michelangelo fled the Medici court before danger came. Making matters worse, his mentor Poliziano had died early in the winter of 1494, giving him all the less incentive to stay. Michelangelo was also influenced by a tale relayed by his good friend, the lute player Cardiere. His friend told him of a vision in which Lorenzo de' Medici warned him that Piero would be driven from the palace. Considering his interest in science, it is surprising that Michelangelo should place any value in such a premonition, but he was always fiercely loyal to his friends. Shortly after Cardiere told him of his vision, Michelangelo departed from Florence with the company of two friends, one of whom is believed to have been Cardiere himself, and their immediate destination was Venice.

Michelangelo's stay in Venice was abbreviated, and the trio left for Bologna. After arriving in the city, they were detained for some sort of violation that required paying a fine of 50 lire. Unable to pay the fine, they were detained, but while this took place, Michelangelo was noticed by local magistrate Gian Francesco Aldrovandi. Michelangelo and his cohorts were freed, and Michelangelo was allowed to stay with Aldrovandi; he had unexpectedly found himself a new patron.

The stay in Bologna also allowed Michelangelo the opportunity to acquaint himself with the native artwork, and he was particularly attracted to the works of Jacopo della Quercia. He enjoyed his time in the new city, but he missed Florence and returned there during the winter of 1495. By this time, the city had stabilized, and Lorenzo di Pierfrancesco de' Medici became his new patron.

Lorenzo commissioned a sculpture of John the Baptist and then one of Cupid, and the latter was the more significant one for Michelangelo. Impressed with his craft, Lorenzo felt that it was up to the standard of ancient sculpture and sold it to Cardinal Riario in Rome. The Cardinal purchased the work under the assumption that it was Ancient, but even after discovering it was not, he was still impressed by Michelangelo's craft. In 1496, he offered him the opportunity to relocate to Rome.

Although Michelangelo was fond of Florence, the city had once again become full of political turmoil. During the mid-1490s, the religious monk Savonarola had risen to popularity, railing against the rule of the Catholic Church and the Medici family. While the city was in conflict, leaving Florence was a prudent decision. Still, Michelangelo's first stay in Rome would prove to be short-lived. Though he didn't care for Cardinal Riario, he worked hard for him, and the sculpture he had been commissioned to complete, *Bacchus* (1496-97), stands as one of his most famous. Ultimately, the work was rejected by Cardinal Riario and instead purchased by Jacopo Galli, a banker and friend.

Bacchus

Considering the acclaim that has since been bestowed upon *Bacchus*, it is remarkable that it was rejected by the Cardinal. However, Cardinal Riario's decision is at least partially understandable because Michelangelo incorporated subversive motifs that would have amounted to blasphemy had it been placed in a church. The god appears almost androgynous, lacking the musculature that was traditionally bestowed upon the gods, and it's easy for viewers to get the sense that his soft body corresponds with soft morals. Even more risqué was the posture of

Bacchus. The vaguely unstable positioning of his feet suggests that he is drunk, a motif substantiated by the rakish contours of his smile and the fact that he clutches a goblet. The raised right leg also establishes a dynamism that broke from the sculptural norms, as the god appears in motion rather than arrested in space. Instead of monumentalizing the god, Michelangelo transformed him into an almost quotidian figure, converting the sacred into the profane.

After he clashed with Cardinal Riario, there was little reason for Michelangelo to remain in Rome, and *Bacchus* was the only work completed during his initial stay in the city. Another determining factor in his decision to leave was that Ludovico's financial troubles had gotten worse, necessitating his son's return. Therefore, in 1497, Michelangelo returned to Florence, where he supported his father, and he would remain there until returning to Rome in 1498.

Despite the fact that his first stay in Rome had been largely unpleasant, Michelangelo returned there after he was commissioned by the Cardinal Jean de Billheres to complete the *Pieta*, which he would finish in 1499. The contract was signed in August of 1498 and agreed to pay him 450 ducats per year. The ambitious agreement stipulated that Michelangelo was to craft a work that "will be the most beautiful work of marble that exists in Rome today, and that no master today could do the work better." That Michelangelo was signed to complete such an ambitious project reflects the acclaim that had already been bestowed upon him by this point in his relatively young career.

The *Pieta* represents one of the most famous works Michelangelo would create in any artistic medium. The large sculpture measures nearly six feet in width and almost seven feet in height, but amazingly the work took Michelangelo less than two years to complete. Similar to his *Crucifix*, his accomplishment lies in his ability to transform relatively standard subject matter into a work of great impact and technical virtuosity. The work was actually one of several that Michelangelo would create of the Pieta theme. The *Pieta* was made from Carrera marble and was to be used for the Cardinal's funeral monument.

Pieta

The *Pieta* had a profound effect upon Michelangelo's contemporaries and even the artist himself, as detailed by an anecdote in Vasari's biography:

"The rarest artist could add nothing to its design and grace, or finish the marble with such polish and art, for it displays the utmost limits of sculpture. Among its beauties are the divine draperies, the foreshortening of the dead Christ and the beauty of the limbs with the muscles, veins, sinews, while no better presentation of a corpse was ever made. The sweet air of the head and the harmonious joining of the arms and legs to the torso, with the pulses and veins, are marvellous, and it is a miracle that a once shapeless stone should assume a form that Nature with difficulty produces in flesh. Michelangelo devoted so much love and pains on this work that he put his name on the girdle crossing the Virgin's breast, a thing he never did again. One morning he had gone to the place to where it stands and observed a number of Lombards who were praising it loudly. One of them asked another the name of the sculptor, and he replied, 'Our Gobbo of Milan.' Michelangelo said nothing, but he resented the injustice of having his work attributed to another, and that night he shut himself in the chapel with a light and his chisels and carved his name on it."

As Vasari indicated, Michelangelo made the unusual act of signing the monument, making it is one of only two works to which he would lend his name. Not only was it unusual for artists to lend their name to a work, but the placement of the signature was controversial as well, since his name appears across Mary's breast-plate. Signing artwork would become more common in subsequent years, but in signing a sculpture of such symbolic subject matter, Michelangelo metaphorically conferred upon himself holy status. This theme is reinforced by the location of the signature. By signing the breast-plate, Michelangelo effectively inserts himself into a central region of the composition, as opposed to customarily signing one's name in the lower right-hand corner.

Despite (or because of) his eclectic formal technique, the sculpture makes a greater impact than it would have had he used a more traditional approach. The technique Michelangelo used for the *Pieta* has been interpreted in a variety of ways, but perhaps the most striking aspect of the composition is the abundance of swirling visual rhythms. There is very little solidity to the composition, which is particularly surprising in light of the fact that the Madonna with Child archetype is a symbolic image of stability. Not only does Christ's body appear flaccid, but the garment worn by Mary appears excessively large, almost to the point of appearing vacuous. For this reason, it has been argued that the sculpture reflects a psychological void, an existential emptiness that is not traditionally found in representations of the Pieta scene throughout Western art.

Another unusual aspect of the *Pieta* is Michelangelo's treatment of the Virgin Mary. Viewing the composition, there is little doubt that Mary laments the loss of her son. However, she appears far too young to convincingly portray the mother of Christ at the time of his death. In fact, she appears even younger than Christ at the time of his death. Considering Michelangelo's emphasis on realism, it comes as a surprise that he should take such a liberty in his depiction of the mother of Christ; some have gone so far as to assert that the facial expression of Mary reproduces that of Christ in Michelangelo's earlier *Crucifix*. With that said, Michelangelo possessed a clear rationale for his highly unusual treatment of Mary; according to Enrico Crispino, "Michelangelo reasoned that the chaste women remain young longer than the not chaste ones; as if he wanted to suggest that Mary's pureness is translated visibly in her everlasting youth". Even with this rationale, it is still shocking to observe the Virgin Mary appearing so youthful at the time of Christ's death.

At the same time, Michelangelo portrays Christ with a heightened degree of naturalism, as his flaccid body appears anatomically correct. In fact, the viewer can infer that the body's anatomical accuracy was no doubt the product of the artist's experiences dissecting bodies in the morgue at Santo Spirito. The *Pieta* thus features a contrast between the apparent realism of

Christ and the less realistic portrayal of Mary. Ultimately, the *Pieta* demonstrates how even when working in sacred, symbolic subject matter, Michelangelo was unafraid to take artistic licenses.

Chapter 5: Back in Florence, 1499-1505

Following the completion of the *Pieta* in 1499, Michelangelo returned to Florence, an indication once again that Michelangelo had no particular attachment to Rome. This time, he would remain in Florence for over five years, staying there until 1505.

The first work that Michelangelo completed upon returning to Florence was *David*, which stands as a tour-de-force in its own right and arguably the most famous work the artist would complete.

David

Although the subject matter was not quite as symbolic as his *Crucifix* or *Pieta*, Michelangelo once again deploys a canonical theme, since his subject represents the famous Biblical figure of the same name. The enormous statue stands 17 feet in height, and in this work Michelangelo exaggerated the proportions of his subject. As a result of the expansive size, the work took him roughly three years to complete, from 1501-1504.

His decision to take on the project was more daring than it might appear retrospectively, because earlier attempts to sculpt the statue had left it maimed, thus transforming it into his most difficult and ambitious work to date. The marble had rested in an uncompleted state for the preceding 25 years, such a long time that there was a certain degree of notoriety to it. It had already been worked on by major artistic figures like Agositno di Duccio and Antonion Rossellino. The rich (and precarious) history of the slab of marble must be taken into consideration when considering why Michelangelo would decide to take on such a difficult project. Always aware of his personal status, Michelangelo would have felt an enhanced sense of pride at successfully completing the project and accomplishing what distinguished artists before him had been unable to finish.

Michelangelo's treatment of the Biblical hero was no less subversive than his past compositions, and even modern viewers are taken aback by the risqué elements of the statue. In particular, one of the most immediately noticeable aspects of the figure is his nudity; David does not wear a loincloth, and he appears entirely unashamed by his nude figure. There is no denying that Michelangelo had been unafraid to feature nudity in his earlier works, like in his *Crucifix*, but it was still controversial to depict a nude figure who was not Christ. In so doing, Michelangelo aligned himself with the Renaissance embrace of the nudity (both male and female) that originally derived from antiquity and served as one of the preeminent tropes of Renaissance art.

Still, even when viewed through the lens of the Renaissance time period, *David* remains iconoclastic, as Michelangelo's treatment of the nude subject differed significantly from that of his contemporaries. First, the figure is quite youthful, not only in facial complexion but also in body type. He is muscular, but it is evident that he lacks the pronounced musculature that is commonly found throughout Renaissance sculpture. Moreover, Michelangelo portrays David in a somewhat sexualized manner; he is not shown in the throes of combat but rather in a passive state. His pensive yet smiling facial expression connotes an air of confidence not only with regard to the battle that is about to take place but also toward his own body. Contemporary viewers would have been startled by the fact that David's penis is uncircumcised, which was unusual during the time period (even if it was not out of place in Renaissance art). There is no reference to the body of Goliath, so the villain's presence is implied rather than explicitly rendered. As a result, his posture forces the viewer to become acutely aware of his frontal nudity, and David's body is the attraction of the statue rather than his battle with Goliath.

Although David's body constitutes a form of spectacle, the mythological connotations of the subject matter are nonetheless of crucial significance. At the turn of the 16th century, Florence had endured nearly a decade of almost persistent political and social turmoil. The death of Lorenzo de' Medici had given way to an incompetent regime captained by Piero de' Medici, and Florence was still in the throes of recovery when Michelangelo returned and began working on the statue. In 1498, the notorious Savonarola had been burnt to death, and the famous city was on the rebound, but commissioning Michelangelo - who by this point was nationally revered for his sculpting abilities - to complete a statue of such magnitude was a major coup for the region. As a Biblical symbol, David perfectly encapsulated the political position of the city, symbolizing the Florentine Republic's defense of its rights. Florence was in an unstable position and remained under constant threat of attack from neighboring city-states. In this vein, it is important to keep in mind that Michelangelo himself was a strong proponent of the Republic, and he welcomed the opportunity to complete a symbol of Florentine strength.

Michelangelo was initially supposed to complete the *David* as part of a series of statues that would adorn the roof of the Florence Cathedral, and Donatello completed one of these statues (depicting the Biblical figure of Joshua) in 1410, an indication of the prolonged duration of the project as a whole. However, the massive size of *David*, which weighed roughly six tons, made it that much more difficult to lift onto a roof. Furthermore, the enormous dimensions meant that the statue needed to be able to be viewed from a wide variety of vantage points. It was not enough to simply view it frontally, as the body has a three-dimensionality that was best appreciated closer to ground level. Besides, the statue deserved to be observed by itself anyway.

It proved difficult to find a location that would do the statue justice. Nine different locations throughout Florence were discussed for the statue, but it was ultimately determined that it would be placed at the entrance of the Palazzo Vecchio. This location was controversial, because it entailed replacing Donatello's sculpture of Judith and Holofernes. Consequently, in the eyes of the city of Florence, Michelangelo had usurped Donatello.

The Palazzo Vecchio in Florence

One of the reasons that the *David* took such a long time to complete was that Michelangelo worked on another project at the same time. From 1501-1504, he also completed niche sculptures for the Piccolomini Altarpiece at the Siena Cathedral in Siena. The altarpiece itself had been commissioned by Cardinal Francesco Todeschini Piccolomini, and the altarpiece was built between 1481-1485 by Andrea Bregno. Michelangelo completed four niche sculptures in total, including *Peter*, *Paul*, *Augustine*, and *Gregory*. The statues may pale in comparison when placed against either the *Pieta* or the *David*, but the niche sculptures are distinguished in their own right. Specifically, Michelangelo broke from tradition by portraying the figures removed from the background of the altarpiece; they exist in an almost three-dimensional space that enhances the realism of the compositions. This naturalistic effect is reinforced by the fact that they do not meet the viewer's gaze directly but instead face different directions. When viewed in the context of their setting, the viewer feels the dynamism of the statues, as though they were alive.

Between 1501 and 1504, Michelangelo also completed one additional project; a Pieta composition entitled *Madonna of Bruges*. The work is so titled due to the fact that it resides in Bruges, and the work makes no actual reference to the Belgian city itself. Considering the subject matter, the work obviously bears similarity with his earlier *Pieta* sculpture. Although she faces forward to a greater extent than in the *Pieta*, in both works Mary dons flowing garments. The major difference between the two is that in the later work, the Virgin Mary is shown with the baby Jesus rather than in his deceased state. Even so, the demeanor and facial complexion of Mary remains virtually unchanged between the two works, highlighting the youthfulness of her appearance in the *Pieta*. While it was more realistic for Mary to appear quite young in *Madonna of Bruges*, her youthfulness is the clear product of artistic license in Michelangelo's earlier work.

Madonna of Bruges

Chapter 6: Between Rome and Florence

Considering his precarious experiences in Rome, one might have reason to expect that Michelangelo would never return to the Ancient city. By 1505, he was 30 years old, a time in which the vast majority of adults had settled into one location and started a family. Michelangelo's resistance to get married or raise children would remain for the rest of his life, and he apparently eschewed intimate contact with anyone. He lived a sparse, ascetic existence akin to a monk, and this is no coincidence. Michelangelo worked in an age in which monks enjoyed great cultural prestige, while artists were generally viewed as artisans. Certainly, Michelangelo was revered, even during the time in which he lived, but one can understand why he felt compelled to behave in the manner of a monk. He ate very little, which allowed his inherently broad-shouldered and athletic physique to become wasted and sullen over time, and he also ignored his own personal hygiene. It is believed that not only did he never bathe but he also wore dog skins on his legs, which he refused to remove for long stretches of time.

Based on this lifestyle, it would stand to reason that he was economically underprivileged, but this was hardly the case. Michelangelo was handsomely compensated for his works and simply refused to spend his money. He held an intense fear of banks and stored all of his money in his living quarters, where he amassed a small fortune. Like his father, he cared a great deal about personal status and money. Where he differed from Ludovico was that Michelangelo possessed an unparalleled work ethic, and he was willing to work tirelessly toward amassing wealth and becoming famous. Instead of tying himself down to a family, Michelangelo was more invested in his work, and he was willing to move if it involved taking on projects of great prestige.

Michelangelo's decision to return to Rome was largely the result of the fact that conditions had changed considerably in the Eternal City by 1505. In 1503, Pope Julius II had succeeded the notorious Alexander VI (Rodrigo Borgia), and Julius II brought an appreciation for the arts to the papacy. After Michelangelo finished the flurry of works that he had worked on during the previous four years, he was commissioned by Pope Julius II to complete a tomb in the Pope's honor. The project was to be massive in scope, and the tomb was to be placed inside of St. Peter's Basilica, the construction of which was intended to take place while Michelangelo designed the tomb.

Michelangelo approached the project with great ambition, delegating a full six months alone to selecting the marble to be used for the tomb. For this task, he traveled to Carrara, a city in the Tuscany region that had been the source for the marble used in many of his earlier works. Michelangelo devoted himself exclusively to the project until 1506, at which point he returned to Rome due to a lack of available money. Consequently, he relocated back to Florence despite having no projects commissioned there, but the temperamental Pope Julius then ordered him back to Rome, threatening to wage war on Florence if he failed to return. With no alternative, Michelangelo returned to Rome later in 1506, but the project was doomed to fail with Pope Julius in command. Julius was suspicious and eventually became consumed with the belief that it was bad luck to have one's tomb built during his lifetime. As a result, the project was aborted altogether in 1508.

Despite terminating the completion of his own tomb, Pope Julius harbored no animosity toward Michelangelo and remained a great admirer of his work. After putting an end to the tomb project, he commissioned Michelangelo to paint the ceiling of the Sistine Chapel, possibly at the goading of Donate Bramante and Raphael, both of whom were jealous of the fame bestowed upon Michelangelo. Although Michelangelo usually relished challenges, Vasari suggests he was reluctant to work on the Sistine Chapel: "Michelangelo tried every means to avoid it, and recommended Raphael, for he saw the difficulty of the work, knew his lack of skill in coloring, and wanted to finish the tomb."

Painting the ceiling of the Sistine Chapel was an undertaking of almost inconceivable proportions. After all, the Sistine Chapel was located in the enormous Papal Chapel in the Vatican, and its immense size posed major challenges, not only with regard to the expansiveness of the ceiling but also due to its height. Being able to reach the ceiling was difficult, and a scaffold constructed from the floor upward to the ceiling would have been unstable. In order to circumvent this difficulty, Michelangelo designed a scaffold built from holes in the wall near the windows, which allowed him increased flexibility and access.

Michelangelo also initially planned to use the assistance of other artists, but perhaps not surprisingly, he felt that inferior artists were not up to his standards. Vasari explained what happened to the other artists he brought from Florence:

"Michelangelo sent to Florence for help, resolving to prove himself superior to those who had worked there before, and to show modern artists the true way to design and paint. The circumstances spurred him on in his quest of fame and his desire for the good of art. When he had completed the cartoons, he waited before beginning to colour them in fresco until some friends of his, who were painters, should arrive from Florence, as he hoped to obtain help from them, and learn their methods of fresco-painting, in which some of them were experienced, namely Granaccio, Giulian Dugiardini, Jacopo di Sandro, Indaco the elder, Agnolo di Donnino and Aristotile. He made them begin some things as a specimen, but perceiving their work to be very far from his expectations, he decided one morning to destroy everything which they had done, and shutting himself up in the chapel he refused to admit them, and would not let them see him in his house. This jest seemed to them to be carried too far, and so they took their departure, returning with shame and mortification to Florence."

The very fact that Michelangelo was able to take on a project of such massive proportions speaks to his versatility as an artist. Very few if any artists would be able to transition from sculpture to painting, particularly in light of the fact that he had not painted in several years. Although his earliest training had been in painting, the training was decades in the past, and he had never completed a painting of any great scope. There was little reason to believe that he was prepared to accomplish a task as great as the ceiling of the Sistine Chapel.

The contract for the Sistine Chapel was signed in May of 1508, and the preliminary stages took a great deal of time. During July and August, five assistants were hired to help with the project; the scaffolding was also established during this time, and in early fall, all of the pigments were sent from Florence. It is believed that the actual painting commenced in either the fall of 1508 or the early months of 1509. Painting began in the entrance and progressed toward the rear.

On an intuitive level, it makes sense to conceive of painting as being less physically demanding than sculpture, but the physical space of the Sistine Chapel posed its own set of difficulties. The work was physically taxing, and an outbreak of mold caused Michelangelo to fall ill and consider giving up the project altogether. Vasari relayed what Michelangelo allegedly told him about the mold:

> "Michelangelo has himself told me that, when he had painted a third of the vault, a certain mouldiness began to appear one winter when the north wind was blowing. This was because the Roman lime, being white and made of travertine, does not dry quickly enough, and when mixed with pozzolana, which is of a tawny colour, it makes a dark mixture. If this mixture is liquid and watery, and the wall thoroughly wetted, it often effloresces in drying. This happened here, where the salt effloresced in many places, although in time the air consumed it. In despair at this, Michelangelo wished to abandon the work, and when he excused himself, telling the Pope that he was not succeeding, Julius sent Giuliano da San Gallo, who explained the difficulty and taught him how to obviate it. When he had finished half, the Pope, who sometimes went to see it by means of steps and scaffolds, wanted it to be thrown open, being an impatient man; unable to wait until it had received the finishing-touches. Immediately all Rome flocked to see it, the Pope being the first, arriving before the dust of the scaffolding had been removed. Raphael, who was excellent in imitating, at once changed his style after seeing it, and to show his skill did the prophets and sybils in the church of Santa Maria della Pace, while Bramante tried to have the other half of the chapel given to Raphael."

After Michelangelo worked at an accelerated pace, the first half of the ceiling was completed in September of 1509, less than a year after starting the painting. At this point, the project was put on hold for a full year, and painting resumed during September of 1510. The second half would ultimately prove more time-consuming than the first, and the ceiling was not completed until October of 1512. Even with the delays, it is remarkable that the painting was completed at such a rapid pace.

Sistine Chapel Ceiling

The *Sistine Chapel* stands as a foremost example of High Renaissance art. The geometric, almost kaleidoscopic rhythms of the composition cohere with the Renaissance emphasis on mathematics and geometric calculus. The ceiling is remarkably complex with regard to both the actual narrative content and the artistic form, and the massive scope makes it difficult to approach as a viewer. To this end, the *Sistine Chapel* ceiling subverted the norms of spectatorship. In his study of the work, Charles Seymour noted, "Ever since its unveiling in 1512, the ceiling has also proved to generations of awed observers a visual puzzle of no small dimension. How was it ever meant actually to be seen? *All at one time?* If not, how and where should one begin to look? And then, how should one proceed? Finally, short of finding an inevitably uncomfortable spot on which to recline on the marble-incrusted pavement of the Chapel, where may one discover the best available point of viewing?"

Seymour identified the visual impact of viewing the *Sistine Chapel Ceiling*. More than any of Michelangelo's works to date, it overwhelms the viewer with its sheer size and virtuoso styling.

In total, nine scenes from the Book of Genesis are conveyed, in addition to 12 prophets and 20 athletic nudes. The most famous of the scenes is the *Creation of Adam*, completed between 1511 and 1512. Viewing the scenes, it is apparent that similar to his earlier works, Michelangelo renders symbolical subject matter esoteric through his eclectic technique. In *Creation of Adam*, the colors are highly saturated. The bodies exhibit a greater degree of musculature than his earlier works, yet their facial expressions and bodily positioning are in line with the exceptional realism of Michelangelo's prior paintings and sculptures. In *Creation of Adam*, God and Adam attempted to lock hands, and the fact that their hands do not actually meet is significant in that it defines the painting as a snapshot in time. In other words, the Biblical figures are not monumentalized but instead appear as relatively ordinary people in motion.

Creation of Adam

Michelangelo also deploys esoteric motifs that confound the viewer, such as the odd collection of bodies behind God grouped together in an unusual, undefined shape that recalls the human brain. Whether or not Michelangelo attempted to reference the brain is ambiguous, but it makes sense when one considers the cultural climate of the Renaissance. In an age when figures like Leonardo da Vinci were preaching the value of scientific and rational thought, it is not difficult to see where Michelangelo would have found the inspiration to incorporate a reference to rational thought in a painting that is otherwise devoted to an archetypal scene from the Bible.

Michelangelo's use of color and nudity in the *Sistine Chapel* are both subversive. Not only are the colors exceptionally saturated (particularly for a fresco painting), but he deploys bright colors that appear almost cartoonish in their intensity. One of the chief examples of this tendency is *The Libyan Sibyl*, one of the 12 prophetic figures.

Libyan Sibyl

The sibyl wears an orange garment, colored with a vibrancy that nearly distracts from the action of the scene depicted. Moreover, the body itself confuses the viewer through its androgyny. There is no method of determining whether it is a male or a female; the musculature would suggest a male, while the garment appears more feminine. In either case, Michelangelo's purpose appears to have been to confound the viewer, another example of the challenging spectatorship dynamics at work with the project.

One of the more subversive aspects of the Sistine Chapel ceiling involves the liberal use of nudity. As noted earlier, nudity was commonly deployed in depictions of Christ, and it became more common during the Renaissance in reference to the gods of antiquity. However, Michelangelo conveys 20 athletic nudes (referred to as *Ignudi*) who possess no apparent symbolic significance. While nudity was relatively common in Renaissance art, Michelangelo's frequent use of nudity appeared gratuitous and certainly subversive in the context of a Papal Chapel. Thus, through its massive scope, esoteric references, color, and nudity, the *Sistine Chapel Ceiling* makes a great impact on the viewer and was particularly risqué at the time of its completion.

Shortly after completing the Sistine Chapel, Pope Julius II passed away. This meant Michelangelo could once again resume progress on the tomb he had begun for Julius years earlier. In 1513, he signed a contract that expanded the scope of the project. Progress was made, but even after working on it for three years, it was not close to completion. In 1516, Julius's sons agreed to a new contract with Michelangelo, but even after that, progress was hardly accelerated. To a degree, the slow pace of the project is due to how devoted Michelangelo was to it; three major sculptures were designed for the tomb, most notably one of Moses. Ultimately, the tomb was not finished in due time, and it remained unfinished for many years. Michelangelo would sign another contract in 1532, and the tomb would not be finished until 1545, about 40 years after it was begun.

Tomb of Pope Julius II

While working on the tomb of Pope Julius II, Michelangelo completed other projects that took him back to Florence on multiple occasions. One notable accomplishment was his design for the Medici Chapel. Between 1520 and 1534, he designed the *New Sacristy*, a mortuary chapel at the Medici Chapel in Florence. Michelangelo designed the tombs for the famous Medici family members, although only two were ever constructed: those of Guiliano di Lorenzo de' Medici and Lorenzo di Piero de' Medici. Eventually, the project was completed, but long after Michelangelo had abandoned it. It was difficult for him to simultaneously balance his work at the Medici Palace in Florence with his efforts at the tomb of Pope Julius II in Rome. Moreover, Florence remained in an unstable political situation, with events such as the attack of Charles V and Pope Clement VII in 1529. These events caused Michelangelo to grow weary of staying in Florence and strongly influenced his eventual decision to permanently relocate in Rome. In the end, the *New Sacristy* reflects his shifting allegiance from Florence to Rome, and it stands as one of several projects that he would work tirelessly on but fail to complete.

Chapter 7: Old Age and Life in Rome

In 1534, Michelangelo was commissioned to complete *The Last Judgment*, a painting that stands behind the altar of the Sistine Chapel, and in 1536 he moved to Rome to complete the assignment. The relocation would prove permanent, and he would remain in the city through his death.

The completion of *The Last Judgment* would take over four years, and the work was not completed until 1541, but Michelangelo sure spent his time wisely. The work stands as Michelangelo's most visually overwhelming work, consisting of a frenzied array of activity. As with the Sistine Chapel ceiling, the viewer has no clear focal point on which to center their attention, and the overall effect is one of chaos. At its most basic level, the fresco depicts the second coming of Christ. People's souls rise and fall according to their final judgment, as determined by Christ and the Saints around him.

The Last Judgment

In many ways, the subversive aspects of the finished work merely build upon the tropes associated with the Sistine Chapel ceiling. Once again, the vast amounts of nudity and bombastic use of color are especially notable. The highly saturated colors stand as an early example of Mannerism, the artistic movement that succeeded the Renaissance. While the Renaissance was committed to rationality and references to antiquity, Mannerism evinced a preoccupation with form that distracted from the subject matter, and this tendency is pronounced in Michelangelo's handling of *The Last Judgment*. Although Michelangelo's portrayal of strong, muscular bodies is commensurate with the Renaissance, his abstract use of shape undercuts the human figures, resulting in a visual overload. His aesthetic eclecticism applies sacred subject matter and renders it almost profane.

The uneasy mixture between the sacred and profane is reinforced by the immense amount of nudity in the fresco, as well as the incorporation of odd, esoteric elements. In fact, the nudity eventually led to the genitalia being covered with drapery following Michelangelo's death in 1564. Meanwhile, one of the more famous examples of Michelangelo's esoteric elements is the flayed skin held by St. Bartholomew. Not only is the flayed body an unusual visual motif, but it has famously been interpreted as a reference to Michelangelo's own body; Michelangelo had not wanted to complete the project and was coerced by Pope Clement VII. St. Bartholomew thus stands as a metaphor for Pope Clement VII's forceful handling of Michelangelo. The facial features correspond with those of Michelangelo, particularly the flattened nose. Moreover, the weightlessness of the flayed skin corresponds with the wasted appearance of the painter himself. Considering his emaciated physique, it is easy to see how he would have been compelled to represent himself in such a manner.

With the completion of *The Last Judgment* in 1541, Michelangelo shifted his focus mainly towards architecture. Although he would complete additional paintings and sculptures in the years leading to his death, his most significant projects late in life involved architecture. The first of these was the Piazza del Campidoglio, which was begun in 1536 and completed a decade later. Unlike his other designs, the Piazzo del Campidoglio entailed designing a plaza rather than a building. The space was of great significance to the city, as it shifted the Roman city center away from the Forum and toward the Papacy. The space is arresting in its spectacle, which includes an enormous statue of Marcus Aurelius, as well as a balustrade and staircase.

Piazza del Campidoglio

In 1546, Michelangelo was commissioned by Pope Paul III to design the *Palazzo Farnese*, which he designed in classic High Renaissance style. The building had first been designed in 1517, and Michelangelo's main accomplishment lay in completing the third story and adding a cornice. He also revised the courtyard.

Unfortunately, the *Palazzo Farnese* is yet another example of a project that was not fully realized. Michelangelo had intended to add a bridge that would connect the palace with the gardens located across the Tiber River, but this added element never came to fruition. Although the bridge would have made the finished product even more overwhelming in its visual grandeur, the *Palazzo Farnese* still exudes the overwhelming impact that characterizes Michelangelo's style.

Palazzo Farnese

The last major project Michelangelo would take on was St. Peter's Basilica, a project that he would begin in 1547 and work on until his death. The building had been erected in the 3rd century A.D., with a redesign that began at the end of the 15th century. For the redesign, famous architects Leon Battista Alberti and Bernardo Rossellino had been commissioned, but they were unable to complete it.

The architectural plan had mainly been devised by Donato Bromante, and Michelangelo drew heavily from his blueprints. By the time Michelangelo began working on the project in 1547, there was a strong design in place but a lack of coherence. Michelangelo's great accomplishment lay in unifying the design, which he achieved through adding a dome atop the ceiling. Furthermore, while Bramante had designed a more regimented pattern of geometric shapes, Michelangelo blurred the harsh geometry, resulting in a more dynamic, flowing appearance. There is a parallel between his handling of the dome and his painting methods. In both cases, he reworked the severe geometry of Renaissance art with a more circular aesthetic that anticipated the Baroque style that would emerge in subsequent decades. Although St. Peter's Basilica would not be completed until 1590, nearly three decades after his death, Michelangelo is credited with designing the dome and is still considered its principal architect.

St. Peter's Basilica

Late in life, Michelangelo continued to lead a quiet, sparse existence. He enjoyed riding his horse and maintained a limited social life. He also wrote a great deal of poetry, mainly sonnets, a practice he had begun earlier in life. Many of these poems contain material that is homoerotic in nature and would have been scandalous, and they are also noteworthy because they suggest that Michelangelo was homosexual, which would at least partly explain his choice to remain unmarried and avoid starting a family.

The poems are challenging to read due to the fact that Michelangelo was largely uneducated. His diction remains coarse, even while his poetic structure and themes are complex. Some scholars speculate that he did develop a relationship that may have been intimate with Vittoria Collonia, but the question of his sexual orientation will forever remain ambiguous. Collonia is believed to have engendered a theological commitment in Michelangelo, but for the most part he lived alone until his physical condition necessitated personal care.

While it's inevitable that people would be interested in the details of a famous artist's life, it's somewhat ironic in the case of Michelangelo because he was so consumed with his work. But some of the most discussed and debated aspects of his life are his relationships with famous contemporaries like Raphael and Leonardo. For example, Vasari wrote almost in passing that Leonardo and Michelangelo had "an intense dislike for each other," leaving others to try to figure out why. One anecdote related in the anonymously authored *Codice Magliabecchiano* may shed light on the topic:

"As Leonardo, accompanied by Giovanni di Gavina, was passing the Spini Bank, near the church of Santa Trinità, several notables were assembled who were discussing a passage in Dante and seeing Leonardo, they asked him to come and explain it to them.

At the same moment Michelangelo passed and, one of the crowd calling to him, Leonardo said: 'Michelangelo will be able to tell you what it means.' To which Michelangelo, thinking this had been said to entrap him, replied: 'No, explain it yourself, horse-modeller that you are, who, unable to cast a statue in bronze, were forced to give up the attempt in shame.' So saying, he turned his back on them and left. Leonardo remained silent and blushed at these words."

While it has long been understood that Michelangelo and Raphael had an unspoken artistic rivalry, Michelangelo's shot across Leonardo's bow, a reference to the fact that Leonardo had never completed an ambitious equestrian statue he was commissioned to complete, remains unexplained. It may simply have been that the ever proud Michelangelo resented the fact that Leonardo was treated like a celebrity wherever he went, despite the fact Leonardo had completed less noteworthy art than he. Since the anecdote does not explain Leonardo's tone, it's impossible to tell whether Michelangelo rightly took offense or simply snapped at him.

Michelangelo eventually died in 1564 at the age of 88, and his life cannot be dissociated from his art. His travels between Florence and Rome were governed more by the projects on which he worked than any personal commitments or attachment to a particular setting. Even though he was born into a large family, he exhibited little affection for them, and for the most part his existence was hermetic. It is remarkable that his career path should have been one chosen almost out of destiny, as he sacrificed his own academic education at a young age in the name of growing as an artist.

Despite his prodigious talent, Michelangelo was fortunate to come of age at a time in which artists enjoyed greater acclaim than ever before. His tenure in the Medici Palace reflects the cultural prestige afforded to artists, and Michelangelo never lacked employment opportunities. His ultimate legacy does not lie in a particular work; instead, Michelangelo's greatest accomplishment is his ability to complete such acclaimed works of art across a variety of different media. Whether painting, sculpting, or designing architecture, Michelangelo engenders a profound response in the viewer, which has led to his famously being named "divine". Achieving success in different art forms makes him the Renaissance artist *par excellence*, rivaled only by the man he apparently detested, Leonardo da Vinci. At the same time, it is also the case that he was unafraid to subvert the norms of Renaissance art, as evidenced by the Sistine Chapel ceiling and *The Last Judgment*. Ultimately, he stands as the rare artist who both personifies a period of art history while also possessing a singular tendency to break from convention.

Bibliography

Bull, George. *Michelangelo: A Biography*. New York: St. Martin's, 1995.

Crispino, Enrico. *Michelangelo*. Firenze: Giunti Gruppo Editoriale, 2001.

Forcellino, Antonio. *Michelangelo: A Tormented Life*. Cambridge: Polity Press, 2009.

Goffen, Rona. *Renaissance Rivals: Michelangelo, Leonardo, Raphael, Titian*. New Haven: Yale University Press, 2004.

Meshberger, Frank Lynn. "An Interpretation of Michelangelo's Creation of Adam Based on Neuroanatomy." *JAMA* 264.14 (1990): 1837-41.

Muntz, Eugene. *Michelangelo*. New York: Parkstone Press, 2005.

Nims, John Frederick. *The Complete Poems of Michelangelo*. Chicago: University of Chicago Press, 2000.

Richardson, Adele. *Michelangelo*. Mankato: Creative Education, 2006.

Seymour, Charles, ed. *Sistine Chapel Ceiling*. New York: W.W. Norton & Company, 1995.

Vogel, Carol. "By the Hand of a Very Young Master?" *New York Times* 12 May 2009.

Wallace, William E. *Michelangelo: Selected Scholarship in English*. Abingdon: Routledge Press, 2005.

Raphael

Chapter 1: A Childhood Filled with Art

"Nature created Michelangelo Buonarroti to excel and conquer in art, but Raphael to excel in art and in manners also." - Vasari

The exact date of birth for Raphael remains ambiguous; it is believed that he was either born on March 28 or April 6, 1481. The date March 28 came from Vasari's claim that he was born on Good Friday that year. Although his date of birth is unclear, the location of his birth is well-documented. Raphael was born in Urbino, a city in the Marche Region of Italy, and his early upbringing was one of great privilege. Raphael was raised in the Urbino court because his father, Giovanni Santi, was employed as an artist there. That Giovanni was allowed to reside in the Urbino court and could count the Duke of Urbino as a patron reflects the high social standing afforded to artists during the early Renaissance. This also ensured that Raphael was exposed to a diverse array of art throughout his own upbringing, as Renaissance society emphasized the importance of music, literature, and painting. Considering these cultural influences, it comes as little surprise that painting would later become Raphael's own profession and livelihood.

Raphael's father had also been raised in a climate of great privilege. Giovanni Santi was himself well-educated, and he not only worked as a painter but also as a poet. In fact, his most recognized achievement was not a painting but instead an epic rhymed poem he completed detailing the life of Federico III da Montefeltro, the Duke of Urbino. He had a strong knowledge of the significant artists of the time period and exposed his son to art from an early age. By today's standards, it may seem shocking that a significant painter would also achieve acclaim as a poet, but Giovanni was a standard-bearer for such artistic versatility, leading one critic to refer to him as the "first painter-poet of the Renaissance" (Goffen 172). In Giovanni's wake, the vast majority of renowned artists throughout the Renaissance, like Leonardo and Michelangelo, excelled across multiple art forms, even if they are now remembered predominantly for their painting.

Although Giovanni was drawn to many different artistic mediums, painting was chief among his passions, and he intended for his son to continue and expand upon the family name in that regard. From the time Raphael was born, Giovanni held great ambition for his son, and his aspirations for his son manifested themselves in multiple ways. The very fact that he named his son Raphael was ostentatious in the context of contemporary Italian society, because Raphael was widely recognized as the most decorated of the archangels (Fraprie). In an even more unique decision, Giovanni refused to hire a wet-nurse to care for his son. During 15th century Italian society, hiring a wet nurse was generally viewed as a marker of socioeconomic privilege, because parents generally did not want to attend to the more "unpleasant" aspects of child-rearing. However, Giovanni's reasoning was not driven by lack of money but instead by a belief that a wet-nurse of lower class would tarnish his son's inherent genius and the social standing that was his birthright. Raphael was instead nursed by his own mother. In his short biography of Raphael, the 16th century artist Vasari described this in ways that sound more comical than anything today: "Giovanni de' Santi, a painter of no great merit, but of good intelligence and well able to show his son the right way, a favour which bad fortune had not granted to himself in his youth. Giovanni, knowing how important it was for the child, whom he called Raphael as a good augury, being his only son, to have his mother's milk and not that of a nurse, wished her to suckle it, so that the child might see the ways of his equals in his tender years rather than the rough manners of clowns and people of low condition."

   The unusual decisions made by Giovanni in regard to his son's upbringing are largely attributable to the fact that Raphael was his only child. By the time Raphael was born, Giovanni was also already past 30 years of age, well older than the point at which men were traditionally expected to have raised a family. In fact, Giovanni was remarkably advanced in age at the time of his wedding as well. While Magia was just 20 years of age, Giovanni was 31, which was middle age based on the standards of the 15th century. Their age discrepancy notwithstanding, it is clear that Giovanni considered his wife to be a suitable parent for his son, likely because Magia was the daughter of an affluent merchant from Urbino, and she demonstrated a degree of sophistication commensurate with Giovanni's own sensibility (Fraprie). Giovanni's desperate attempt to raise Raphael into a famous artist was also due to the fact that he and his wife had conceived of two children (a boy and a girl) prior to the birth of Raphael, but they had each died while still in infancy. For this reason, Giovanni was desperate for a son to carry on the family name, realizing that Raphael represented his last - and only - means through which to continue and further his own legacy.

   The cultural and artistic climate of Italy during the late 15th century greatly explains the environment in which Raphael would later work and illuminates the reasons why Giovanni was especially driven to raise an heir to what he saw as his artistic legacy. By the late 1400s, Italian society had already turned away from the medieval emphasis on the Church demonstrated through the Byzantine art of the past several centuries. With the arrival of painters like Giotto and Cimabue, it once again became popular to emphasize emotion and color in art, and the monochromatic, gold palette characteristic of Byzantine art was replaced by colorful frescoes and paintings that effectively told complex narratives. Additionally, with the arrival of mathematically-inclined figures like Giovanni Battista Alberti, art evinced a commitment to symmetry and scientific worldliness that had previously been absent. By the end of the last decade of the 15th century, Leonardo and Michelangelo had already become widely recognized throughout the country. Leonardo's *Last Supper*, completed in 1494, had a profound impact on Raphael's career, as would his later masterpiece *The Mona Lisa* (1503-1506). Meanwhile, Michelangelo completed his early crucifixes and famous *Pieta* during the decade as well. With such innovative artistic luminaries gaining public recognition while Raphael was being raised, Raphael could not have grown up in a more opportune time.

Considering the rigorous attempts to document the life of Raphael following his premature death, it is surprising that there is a relative dearth of knowledge about Raphael's early upbringing. Much of what has historically believed to have been true about his childhood may in fact be largely apocryphal, and the true story of his upbringing will never be definitively affirmed. However, what is certain is that Raphael was raised in an environment filled with art, because Giovanni lived and worked in the institution of Urbino known as *Il Corte* during his early years. It's unclear whether Raphael actually received any formal instruction as a young child, but Vasari wrote that Raphael was allowed to work on art with his father: "When the boy was grown, Giovanni began to teach him painting, finding him much inclined to that art and, of great intelligence. Thus Raphael, before many years and while still a child, greatly assisted his father in the numerous works which he did in the state of Urbino."

Fortunately for Raphael, this was not a problem, as Giovanni was more than capable of offering skilled instruction. Giovanni operated an artistic workshop in the Urbino Court that mainly produced materials for entertainment functions, and though Giovanni would pale in comparison to his famous son as an artist, Raphael received a comprehensive art education from him. In addition to producing art, Giovanni was a devout art enthusiast who exposed his young son to a wide array of painters, some of whom would impact Raphael's mature style. Giovanni's favorite artists included Leonardo, Mantegna, Signorelli, and the Dutch master Jan Van Eyck (Fraprie). Most usefully, Raphael learned from his father not only learned to appreciate art but also how to absorb different techniques and apply them in practice.

Van Eyck's self-portrait

Raphael's early upbringing was thus one of great satisfaction and pleasure. However, in 1491, when he was still just 8 years old, his mother died. During the time period, men were expected to remain married throughout their adult lives, and Giovanni wasted little time in remarrying. His second wife, Barnadina Parta, was remarkably similar to his first one. Like Magia, she was the daughter of a wealthy merchant, but apart from her financial affluence, Giovanni's reasons for marrying her remain unclear. The pair was never close, and Barnadina demonstrated little interest in raising her stepson. She and Giovanni would not have a child together, and Barnadina treated Raphael with indifference. At the time, however, divorce was deeply frowned upon, so this awkward family dynamic continued unchanged until 1494. That year, when Raphael was a young teen, Giovanni died. While it is true that life expectancy was far shorter during the 1400s than it is today, it is still uncanny that he lost both of his parents at such a young age. In the span of three years, his life had been completely transformed, shifting from a life of extreme comfort to orphan status. Making matters worse, it quickly became clear that Raphael's stepmother held little interest in continuing to raise her stepson, so it was necessary for Raphael to find a new family with which to live. His formal guardian became his uncle Bartolomeo, who served as a priest. That made Bartolomeo an untenable parent, and young Raphael was suddenly left with no interested caretaker.

Chapter 2: Life as an Apprentice

While it is certain that Raphael continued to work as an artist following the deaths of his parents, it is unclear where he worked or received training. It has historically been suggested that Giovanni arranged for his son to serve as an apprentice to the famous Pietro Perugino, a famous artist across Italy and a personal favorite of Giovanni's. Vasari claimed:

> "At last this good and loving father perceived that his son could learn little more from him, and determined to put him with Pietro Perugino, who, as I have already said, occupied the first place among the painters of the time. Accordingly Giovanni went to Perugia, and not finding Pietro there he waited for him, occupying the time in doing some things in S. Francesco. When Pietro returned from Rome, Giovanni being courteous and well bred, made his acquaintance, and at a fitting opportunity told him what he wished in the most tactful manner. Pietro, who was also courteous and a friend of young men of promise, agreed to take Raphael. Accordingly Giovanni returned joyfully to Urbino, and took the boy with him to Perugia, his mother, who loved him tenderly, weeping bitterly at the separation."

There is a lot of skepticism about Vasari's account, because it would suggest that Raphael had entered a formal apprenticeship when he was younger than 11, something that would have been almost unheard of by the standards of contemporary Italian society. Scholars now believe that Raphael did not enter such an apprenticeship until several years later. Raphael was certainly a precocious talent, but the standards of the time period suggest that his apprenticeship began closer to the end of the decade. Instead of joining Perugino before his father's death, it is likely that Raphael was tutored by a local artist of some acclaim while he continued to reside in the Urbino court. Following the death of his father, he likely lived with his stepmother for a short time while he operated his father's workshop.

That Raphael was able to successfully run his father's workshop attests to his prodigious skill, and it was not long before the young Raphael garnered a strong reputation throughout the city for his skill. It was unusual for a young artist to run a workshop before having undergone a formal apprenticeship, and as a result, Raphael was not yet perceived of as a master. This makes even more sense considering the fact that even though he remained busy as an artist and had been exposed to more great works than most young artists his age, he was still largely self-taught at this age.

Given his immense talent, it was only a matter of time before Raphael was taken under the wing of a recognized manner, and regardless of when it happened, he did become an apprentice to Pietro Perugino. It is likely that the move occurred around 1498, when Raphael was 15 years of age. By this time, he was at an appropriate age to serve an apprenticeship, and he would have needed formal instruction in order to advance his career. That his father had extolled the virtues of Perugino's art no doubt assured the teenager that Perugino's tutelage would have a productive effect on his artistic education. The apprenticeship would also drastically alter the trajectory of his career by providing instruction from a master and the opportunity to work on projects of greater scope than he had while running his father's workshop in Urbino.

Pietro's self-portrait (circa 1497-1500)

Raphael's new apprenticeship required relocating to Perugia, where Perugino worked and resided. Perugia was vastly dissimilar to Urbino, with both a significantly different geographic and sociopolitical situation. The capital city of Umbria (and to the south of Urbino), Perugia is located on a tall hilltop of far greater elevation than Urbino. The natural setting remains more dramatic than Urbino, but during the 15th century, Perugia was engulfed in political turmoil. The city was under the rule of popes who were unable to police the landscape, and the shift from the peacefulness of Urbino to the conflict of Perugia came as a shock to the young Raphael.

Despite the current of disorder, however, Perugia held clear advantages over Urbino. It was (and remains) a center for artistic production throughout the Renaissance. Perugia was also home to a university, and there were a relatively large amount of educated people calling Perugia home at the time. For someone who grew up in a household that emphasized humanistic thought and placed a premium on artistic endeavors, Perugia offered great appeal for Raphael.

Raphael spent roughly four years in the studio of Perugino, and the influence of Perugino is clear in a number of different ways. First, Perugino's main trademark lay in his ability to harmonize compositions through mathematically correct compositions (Gardner). Viewing Perugino's works, it becomes immediately apparent that the master painter had studied the developments made by Leon Battista Alberti and other forerunners of the Italian Renaissance. For example, in his most famous work, *The Delivery of the Keys* (1481-82), Perugino deploys a strict mathematical calculus that reflects an awareness of the developments made in Renaissance perspective by artists earlier in the century. Filippo Brunelleschi is often cited as the first artist to use "linear perspective," which can best be described as painting a firsthand view of what an artist sees from his angle. Instead of having the painting's subjects perfectly centered, the perspective style often places subjects off center, and the size of objects decreases in proportion to how far away from the viewer they appear. To fully accomplish "linear perspective," Renaissance artists used painting techniques to give their works a three-dimensional appearance by mixing colors, through lighting and shading. They also angled their subjects differently to make them appear closer or farther away in the painting, a technique known as foreshortening. Some of the best examples of linear perspective artwork can be found in Melozzo da Forli's frescoes at the Basilica della Santa Casa in Loreto, Italy, in which the viewer's perspective is angled as though they are on the ground looking up at the subjects of the painting. Da Forli knew his work would be viewed by people on the ground looking up at the work, and what makes linear perspective so effective is that the artist can create ideal angles if he or she knows the angle at which actual viewers will be viewing the work, making the art appear much more lifelike.

In Perugino's painting, Saint Peter is given the keys to the kingdom of heaven, a Biblical scene taken from Matthew: 16. That Perugino chose to paint this scene is not unusual, but the formal methodology is, because Perugino hierarchically divided the image into three distinct planes, all united by a rotunda at the center of the rear plane. There is no clear main character, as the artist emphasizes spatial fidelity at the hands of privileging any of the characters. The geometric accuracy of the composition lends a heightened realism to the work, as though the scene was a reasonable representation of the famous Biblical episode.

The Delivery of the Keys

In addition to being one of the first artists to accurately implement Renaissance perspective, Perugino also stands as one of the initial painters to use oil as a material. The turn toward oil painting marked a clear departure from the fresco paintings completed by figures like Giotto and Cimabue. Fresco paintings had popularized early Renaissance art, but since oil dried less quickly, it afforded artists the time to work more carefully and deliberately. Unlike fresco, the artist was also no longer tied to a particular setting and could work from the comfort of an easel. From the beginning, Raphael would borrow from his instructor, and despite completing frescoes on a number of occasions, oil would generally remain his medium of choice throughout his career.

As was customary during the late 15th century, apprentices lived with their masters, and the relationship between teacher and pupil was extremely close. With the relatively recent death of his father, it is evident that Perugino became a surrogate father to Raphael. At the same time, working in such close contact with the Perugian master meant that Raphael's style became virtually indiscernible from that of his teacher. On the one hand, this gave him a clear understanding of Perugino's technique and how to produce works of immense skill. But on the other hand, copying the style of Perugino carried the necessary limitation of restricting Raphael's style to that of his teacher. After all, the majority of assignments undertaken by Raphael during his apprenticeship were commissions that had been awarded to Perugino, and the Italian master needed to deliver finished products that were commensurate with both his significant skill and his singular artistic style. Ultimately, the dynamics between artist and pupil make it virtually impossible to discern the earliest work of Raphael from that of Perugino. As one scholar noted,

"The comradeship of artists and the relations of master and pupil were so intimate that we are today at a loss absolutely to separate their work in all cases. This is not strange when we consider that the first task set to a pupil was the copying of drawings by his master." (Fraprie 22).

Moreover, the influence of Perugino on Raphael's artwork was not limited to his apprenticeship but also extended to Raphael's own mature works. The challenge of distinguishing between works completed by Raphael and those done by Perugino complicates questions of authorship. If nobody can discern the works of the two artists, it is difficult to declare Raphael the true "author" of the works he completed under Perugino. At the same time, everyone can acknowledge the productive, nurturing influence of Perugino in the gradual formation of Raphael's own artistic style. Ultimately, Raphael's training attests to the strong importance of the master-apprentice relationship within Renaissance society, as well as the shared formal and thematic interests between Raphael and his teacher.

One famous example of the largely undistinguishable relationship between Raphael's earliest works and those of his teacher can be seen in his *Resurrection of Christ* (1499-1502). Although it has been argued that this work was in fact Raphael's first commissioned work after leaving the studio of Perugino, it is likely that it was begun before the close of the century, and therefore while he was still under the tutelage of his master instructor. If an art scholar was told that *Resurrection of Christ* was completed by Perugino, it is unlikely that they would be surprised, as there are many formal and thematic similarities borrowed from Perugino. First, the painting showcases the clearly defined characters and expert symmetry that could only have been gleaned from the instruction of his teacher. As with Perugino, the composition is remarkably complex, with a flurry array of activity that is notable for its geometric regularity. Furthermore, the saturated colors borrow heavily from Perugino, including the almost cartoonish incorporation of purple, orange, and green. Even contemporary artists of the time could not distinguish between Raphael's earliest works and Perugino's, as Vasari noted: "When Pietro had seen Raphael's method of drawing and his fine manners and behaviour, he formed an opinion of him that was amply justified by time. It is well known that while Raphael was studying Pietro's style he imitated him so exactly in everything that his portraits cannot be distinguished from those of his master, nor indeed can other things, as we see in some figures done in oils on a panel in S. Francesco at Perugia for Madonna Maddalena degli Oddi."

Resurrection of Christ

It is necessary to recognize that the reasons Raphael borrowed heavily from his instructor were not only a natural result of his education process but also commercial. For this reason, it has been noted that even though "Raphael in later years greatly departed from the stereotyped formulas, his Perugian work shows him as still an adherent to the old types, which his Umbrian customers doubtless required" (Fraprie 31). Despite the fact that *Resurrection of Christ* was not actually completed by Perugino himself but rather by Raphael, the master deserves mention, since his influence is unmistakable throughout the work.

While *Resurrection of Christ* bears the imprint of Perugino, it also reveals Raphael gradually moving away from the style of his master. In particular, there is notably more dynamism to the composition than in *The Delivery of the Keys*. Where Perugino's work involves virtually no interaction between the planes of the image, Raphael establishes an almost flowing rhythm throughout. Christ stands at the center of the composition, flanked by three figures on each side;

each character gestures toward Jesus, not only implicitly signaling his importance but also creating an interrelated connection between the people and elements of the composition. This flowing rhythm also appears through the bodies of the figures themselves, which contain a curving posture. Indeed, all of the bodies appear in motion, a clear departure from the stolid rhythms of Byzantine and early Renaissance art. Raphael's combination between clearly regulated symmetry and the dynamism of his characters makes this early work a forerunner for the High Renaissance and a precursor to the paintings completed by Michelangelo in the following century.

Regardless of the exact date in which Raphael entered Perugino's studio, he remained under the tutelage of his instructor for an extended period of time. However, after the first few years of the 16th century, it became clear that Raphael had equaled or even surpassed the talents of his master. Indeed, by the age of 17 in 1500, it was already commonplace for Raphael to be referred to as a *maestro* (master) (Strinati). During Renaissance Italy, for a painter to work independently meant that they had already demonstrated skill commensurate with the lofty standards of their instructor, a process that entailed years of training.

Even though Raphael had achieved the requisite mastery to work for himself by 1500, Raphael remained in the studio of Perugino for several years. But Raphael was still permitted to complete commissions for himself, and he would remain remarkably prolific throughout the rest of his life. Raphael's first commissioned work was the Baronci Altarpiece, an oil painting completed from 1500-1501 in the chapel of the church of Sant'Agostino in Citta di Castello, located close to Urbino. Although the commission was delegated to both Raphael and another painter, the elder Evangelista da Pian de Meleto, Raphael assumed control over its completion and remains the painter associated with the work (Fraprie).

An angel that was part of the altarpiece painting

    The Baronci Altarpiece was a monumental undertaking, but unfortunately, the church in which it was housed was stricken by an earthquake during the 18th century, making it impossible to determine exactly how the finished painting appeared. What is known is that there were at least six components to the work, including two angels, two images of Saint Nicholas of Tolentino, an image of the Virgin Mary, and another of God. Each of these images was relatively small, but together they comprised a project of significant ambition, particularly for a young artist such as Raphael.

    Although it was an ambitious project, it is still apparent that the work lacks the polish of his later, more famous works. In fact, Roma Goffen goes so far as to argue, "Raphael's earliest paintings allow no intuition of his future. Nothing in his first undisputed work the altarpiece of San Nicolo Tolentino commissioned for the church of Sant'Agostino in Citta di Castello…anticipates his future achievements…Raphael is art's greatest paradox, at once eclectic and original." (171). But the argument that the Baronci Altarpiece bears no resemblance to Raphael's later works seems more than a bit excessive, and it could even be argued that the work is more closely aligned with his mature style than his *Resurrection of Christ*. In particular, Raphael places greater emphasis on the faces of his subjects in this work, anticipating the numerous portraits he would later complete. Moreover, the soft, almost effeminate features of the characters are commensurate with his later works as well. On a thematic level, the theme of Saint Nicholas with the Devil at his feet is also not dissimilar to his later *St. George and the Dragon* (1504-06). The Baronci Altarpiece does not contain the bravura mathematical rigor of Raphael's more famous compositions, but there are still significant similarities with his later works.

One of Raphael's most significant developments during the earliest years of the 16th century was that he began completing more small-scale paintings, including a series of portrayals of patron saints. The first among these was *Saint Sebastian*, a very small work commissioned and completed between 1501 and 1502. Considering that portraiture is one of Raphael's defining genres, the painting is inherently of great significance, and in many ways, *Saint Sebastian* set the standard for his style of portraiture. The soft facial expression of the patron saint is commensurate with his later works, as Raphael transforms the masculine saint into an effeminate, largely androgynous figure. Also of note are the fingers of Saint Sebastian, most notably the pinky, which stands apart from the rest of his fingers in a gentle manner. The delicateness with which Raphael conveys the saint reflects the formidable spirituality of the figure, adhering to the theme that delicateness connotes spiritual piety.

Saint Sebastian

Although *Saint Sebastian* is in many ways similar to Raphael's later works, the painting still bears the influence of Perugino and does not possess the sophistication of his subsequent portraits. Notably, there is no incorporation of the atmospheric *sfumato* touches that would characterize later Raphael paintings, and the end result looks somewhat simplistic. The most complex component to the work is the finger contortion of Saint Sebastian, yet the painting also lacks the realistic tonal gradations that would imbue it with a more realistic appearance.

The most significant work completed by Raphael between 1500 and 1504 was the Oddi Altarpiece, commissioned for the altar of the Oddi chapel in San Francesco al Prato in Perugia. The complete work, which contains both the altarpiece proper and a predella, portrays the crowning of the Virgin Mary, and the scenes of the annunciation, the arrival of the magi, and the presentation of the baby Jesus to the Virgin Mary. The work was enormous, both in scope and in size, and though the cluttered composition recalls the works of Perugino, the incorporation of such a vast number of scenes qualifies the Oddi Altarpiece as Raphael's most ambitious project to date. In the altarpiece itself, there are two levels. On the top one, the Virgin Mary is crowned; meanwhile, on the bottom part the apostles are shown with Mary's tomb, with Saint Thomas clutching the girdle. On each level, there is an almost overwhelming array of activity. Behind Mary, a flurry of angels is shown, together comprising an ornamental motif that makes the altarpiece nearly bombastic in its decorative elements. Similar to his *Saint Sebastian*, Raphael refrains from including any tonal gradations, so the composition is not particularly realistic. Still, the altarpiece is stylistically remarkable for its use of symmetry, as characters are positioned in parallel groupings that again reflect the Renaissance emphasis on mathematical accuracy.

The upper section depicts the crowning of the Virgin Mary, and the lower section depicts St. Thomas holding Mary's girdle after her body rose to Heaven.

The Oddi Altarpiece was not completed until 1504, and while much of this can be attributed to the massive scope of the project, the protracted length is also due to the fact that Raphael worked on other paintings concurrently. Between 1500 and 1504, he led a relatively nomadic existence, shifting back and forth between Urbino, Perugia, and towns in between the two cities. One of Raphael's most famous works from this early period was his *Mond Crucifixion*, completed between 1502 and 1503. The work was commissioned by the church of San Domenico in Citta di Castello (near Urbino), and it is massive in its own right. The relatively standard scene portrays Jesus on the crucifix, flanked by two angels to his immediate right and left, and a gathering of four individuals seated below on the ground. The altarpiece constitutes an apparent departure from the business of the *Oddi Altarpiece*, as it is far more measured and restrained in its design.

Mond Crucifixion

As with Raphael's earlier works, however, there is a programmatic use of space, as each of the figures are carefully positioned in a symmetrical design. The two angels are positioned directly opposite from one another, and the four figures on the ground reproduce the parallel grouping. On the left are the Virgin Mary and Saint Jerome (the saint for whom the altarpiece was dedicated), while the right-hand side of the painting portrays Mary Magdalene with John the Evangelist in the background. The parallel composition is not only aesthetically in tune with the artistic trends of the Renaissance but includes thematic resonance as well. By grouping three figures to Jesus' right and left, Raphael affirms that Christ is the clear subject of the work, and this makes his appearance more dramatic than if he were interacting with the other characters. Another notable aspect of the *Mond Crucifixion* is that Raphael signed the work, which not only asserted himself as the author but demonstrated a clear sense of artistic confidence and pride in the work. Although the characters do not have the monumental solidity that would characterize Raphael's later renderings of human figures, the signature and geometric emphasis signal Raphael's own confidence as an artist and the development of his style.

The *Oddi Altarpiece* and the *Mond Crucifixion* demonstrate how one of Raphael's chief interests during his early career involved crucifixion scenes. At the same time, Raphael became fascinated by the symbol of the Madonna, a development that can perhaps be attributed to Leonardo's completion of the *Mona Lisa* (1503-06). While it is uncertain exactly when Raphael first became exposed to the *Mona Lisa*, one can be certain that he was familiar with the works of Leonardo, and he likely would have known that Leonardo was working on the painting. The similarities between Raphael's Madonnas and the *Mona Lisa* are more formal in nature than thematic; after all, the *Mona Lisa* does not portray a spiritual figure but instead a simple Italian woman. But even if Raphael's focus is more spiritual than Leonardo's works, his compositions borrow from the geometric calculus and monumental stability of Leonardo's designs.

The first of Raphael's Madonnas was his *Solly Madonna*, which was completed sometime between 1500 and 1504. As it was painted during the time in which Raphael was still in the orbit of Perugino, it naturally bears the imprint of his former teacher. The religious subject matter, the soft features of the Virgin Mary, and her extraordinarily strong mouth all gesture toward the style of Perugino. Additionally, as with Perugino, Raphael portrays the bodies of both the baby Jesus and the Virgin Mary as soft and fleshy, in stark contrast with the style of Leonardo, Michelangelo, or the artists of the High Renaissance. When viewing the composition, viewers immediately notice that the infant's body appears almost flabby in its proportions, and the Virgin Mary appears particularly soft as well. Throughout the history of Western art, the soft body has been popular during certain periods, but the Renaissance was committed to the revitalization of antiquity, and it became popular to depict bodies as strong and muscular. In 1490, Leonardo had completed his *Vitruvian Man*, which set the standard for the strong, muscular bodies that were popular over the next century.

Solly Madonna

If the body type of the Virgin Mary and the Baby Jesus differ greatly from the conventions of the time period, it is still evident that Raphael was absorbing the influence of Leonardo. This is most clearly expressed through the three-quarter pose adopted by the Virgin Mary, as though she posed for a portrait. Moreover, the relatively small dimensions of the painting (measuring just 20 x 15 inches) were also significant; by rendering such symbolic subject matter on a small scale, Raphael effectively transposed the most sacred theme in Western art to the dimensions of secular portraiture. While this might superficially appear to debase the name of one of the most holy figures, portraying the Virgin Mary on a small scale only makes her more appealing and approachable. Indeed, when the mother of Christ is positioned in an enormous altarpiece, she is viewed from a great distance and it becomes difficult to identify with her on an intimate level. Paradoxically, by painting Mary in the same manner that one would a portrait, Raphael actually brought her closer to the viewer. Instead of resonating as a distant Biblical figure, the viewer views her in the same terms that one would view their own mother, thereby ensuring that the mother of Christ assumes the role of a universal mother. In the end, that work, and Raphael's subsequent Madonna compositions, exemplifies Raphael's deft balance between the sacred and the secular, and his ability to synthesize elements of each within a harmonious composition.

In some ways, Raphael's subsequent Madonnas follow in the same vein as the *Solly Madonna*. Two of Raphael's best-known Madonna paintings are his *Connestabile Madonna* (1502-04) and *Madonna and Child with the Book* (1503). It is perhaps surprising that the title of the latter painting makes specific reference to a book, since the incorporation of a book is a recurring theme throughout each of the Madonna paintings. The rationale behind including the book is unclear. In any event, the motif is not faithful to the time period in which Christ lived, since there was no printing press in existence. Ultimately, it is most appropriate to interpret the book similarly to the portrait size, since both are motifs that transform the Virgin Mary and baby Jesus into figures relatable to a contemporary audience. By holding a book, it is implicitly acknowledged that Mary understands how to read, a feat that (in the context of Renaissance Italy) connoted worldly knowledge. By reading to her son, Mary not only asserts that she has received an education but demonstrates that she intends to teach her son how to read and become a citizen of the world.

While Raphael's renderings of the bodies themselves were slightly anachronistic by the time in which the Madonna paintings were made, the themes that resonate throughout them were progressive and unforeseen in religious painting. Raphael not only demonstrates a commitment to cherished religious symbols but manages to integrate developments in contemporary Italian society within a religious framework. Instead of a binary between humanistic inquiry and religious symbol, he successfully combines the two into a composition that is well-balanced and manages to avoid disorienting the viewer. In this end, what the Madonna paintings abdicate with regard to historical fidelity they gain in accessibility. Perhaps more than any other artist, Raphael can be credited with making religious figures easily relatable.

Connestabile Madonna

One of the final works Raphael completed while still in Perugia was *The Marriage of the*

Virgin, finished in 1504. The project was originally intended for Perugino to complete, but Raphael's former instructor relayed the assignment to Raphael, and he finished the painting during his final months in Perugia. It is not difficult to understand why Perugino would have been commissioned to complete the painting, since it is evident that the patron wanted it painted in the style of Perugino's famous *The Delivery of the Keys*. In this regard, the painting is an example of how effectively Raphael was able to copy the style of his old teacher. The painting was the third that Raphael would complete for the church in Citta di Castello, all of which were completed in the style of Perugino. Most noticeably, the paintings contain a clear demarcation between foreground and background space, with the spatial systems unified through the rotunda that occupies the back of the painting.

The Marriage of the Virgin

At the same time, Raphael's use of perspective is far more sophisticated than his master's use of it. In his seminal biography of Raphael, Vasari noted that in *The Marriage of the Virgin*, there "may be distinctly seen the progress of excellence of Raphael's style, which becomes more subtle and refined, and surpasses the manner of Pietro. In this work…there is a temple drawn with such care that it is marvellous to behold the difficulty of the problems which he has there set himself to solve." With Pietro's composition, the rotunda in the background is not clearly connected to the figures in the foreground, but Raphael achieves the connection by conspicuously outlining the rows of steps, which magnify the vanishing point of the image and achieve true Renaissance perspective. While Raphael would depart from the Perugino-inspired style of *The Marriage of the Virgin*, the work stands as an excellent example of Raphael's technical virtuosity.

Chapter 3: Florence

By 1504, Raphael had been recognized and established as a significant artist in his own right. However, he was still associated with Perugino, not only because of the obvious formal similarities between their respective styles but because they operated in close proximity. While Raphael would continue to hold his former teacher as a major influence on his career, there was nothing preventing him from leaving the Umbrian capital. Similar to his father, he had eschewed starting a family in his 20s. In fact, Raphael would remain unmarried his entire life.

Considering that he possessed no commitments requiring him to remain in Perugia, it should come as little surprise that Raphael moved to Florence in 1504. Just as his move to Perugia had been motivated by artistic opportunities, Raphael's relocation to Florence was due to the burgeoning art scene that had erupted in the Italian city now most associated with the Renaissance (Bossy, Brothers, and McEnroe). Florence was already one of the major outposts for the High Renaissance, and by the time Raphael arrived, both Leonardo and Michelangelo were situated in the city. For the 23 year-old Raphael, the opportunity to work in the same place as those two masters was an alluring opportunity, and there were also a wealth of opportunities to remain well-employed by completing paintings for local patrons.

Raphael was already well aware of the works of both Leonardo and Michelangelo, who had collectively galvanized the High Renaissance through vastly different means. While Leonardo was invested in science and rational thought, Michelangelo was far more emotional and introspective in his work. Both artists were committed to the life of the mind, yet Leonardo took a more scientific, intellectual emphasis that contrasted with Michelangelo's more philosophical perspective. The contrast between the two Renaissance giants also surfaces through their formal technique. Leonardo's art is defined by its scientific bent and geometric accuracy, while Michelangelo showcased a more flowing, curved aesthetic. Although Raphael was more heavily influenced by Leonardo, one can observe the influence of both artists throughout his career.

It is important to recognize that while Raphael's fame would later equal (and even contemporarily surpass) Leonardo and Michelangelo, at the time of his arrival in Florence, his reputation was parasitic in comparison. As one write put it, "When Raphael arrived in the city in 1504, despite his social connections and considerable accomplishments, he posed little threat to anyone, and certainly not to Michelangelo, then enjoying his first great public triumph with the

David' (Goffen 183). Michelangelo finished the *Pieta* in 1498, and given that 1504 saw the completion and public release of his famous statue *David*, there was no more decorated artist in Florence than Michelangelo. Furthermore, Leonardo had already completed his *Vitruvian Man* and *Last Supper* by 1504, and he had either completed or nearly finished the *Mona Lisa*. That Raphael was even able to insert himself into an artistic climate that was so heavily dominated by two figures reflects the magnitude of his own artistic talents.

Two ways in which Raphael was able to further his own reputation was through carving a niche for himself in portraiture and continuing to complete Madonna paintings. These two genres were not as dissimilar as they might seem, since Raphael's Madonna paintings borrowed heavily from the conventions of portraiture. When viewing his works from this period, it is easy to discern a consistent style, characterized by solid, clearly defined forms and delicate features. Raphael continued to display a singular ability to fuse the secular with the sacred.

Although Raphael had largely resisted portraiture during his time in Perugia, he actually completed his first proper portrait while working there: a portrait of Pietro Perugino. Considering the deep bond between Raphael and his former teacher, it is striking that he portrays Perugino in terms that are not especially flattering. The old master is shown with a serious expression bordering on a scowl, and his thick features are not particularly attractive. His soft body is also notably different from the hard, muscular physiques that typified Renaissance art. Raphael's Perugino is not only physically unattractive but also exudes little of the intellectual brilliance that the artist presumably possessed. One can infer that Raphael felt a great sense of reverence for his former teacher, but this is not apparent in the portrait. Instead, his concern appears to have been to capture Perugino as realistically as possible, and that may have been what Perugino himself desired. The portrait raises the issue of whether the artist has a greater responsibility to portray his subject in realistic or ideal terms, and it is clear that Raphael was committed to the former approach.

Raphael's portrait of Perugino

The portraits Raphael completed during his Florentine period similarly eschew the musculature of most Renaissance art. One of his earliest Florentine portraits was a self-portrait, which remains one of his most famous works and is in stark contrast to the portrait he made of Perugino. While Pietro has hard features and wears a frown, Raphael portrays himself with remarkably soft features, long hair, and beautiful eyes. At the same time, his appearance differs sharply from the Renaissance standards. While he does not have the flabbiness of Pietro, he also possesses none of the hard muscularity that typified Renaissance art. Raphael appears almost androgynous, and on first glance his long hair and long gaze appear quite effeminate. The reasons for conveying himself in such feminine terms are ambiguous, especially because the absence of photographs makes it impossible to determine exactly how Raphael actually appeared. However, Raphael appears to have borrowed from his Madonna paintings when designing his own countenance, as the ovular cheeks and soft eyes appear closer to his earlier paintings than to the masculine norms of the time period. Though his portrayal may fall short of contemporary masculine standards, Raphael's portrait depicts himself as more "beautiful" than "handsome."

The self-portrait of Raphael is also significant in that it reflected the rise of the artist as a prestigious figure in society. In previous eras, portraiture was reserved for royalty or religious figures, and through painting himself Raphael placed himself on the same level as the socially revered subjects who could afford to pay to have their portrait painted. Through valorizing the profession of the artist, Raphael also followed in the wake of other noted artists, such as Jan Van Eyck and Albrecht Durer. Van Eyck's self portrait, ambiguously titled *Portrait of a Man* (1433), conveys him looking sternly yet wisely in the direction of the viewer. His appearance carries an understated virtuosity that implicitly lent an air of respectability to the artist as a social figure. Even though Van Eyck was Dutch, he was a favorite artist of Giovanni Santi, and his self-portrait would almost certainly have been in Raphael's mind while completing his own self-portrait. Meanwhile, Durer's *Self Portrait* was completed just four years before Raphael's, and given that the two artists were well-acquainted, Raphael was likely familiar with the work (Sweetser). Durer's painting is even more effusive than either that of Raphael or Van Eyck in its celebration of the artist. In fact, his long hair and pious expression bear a strong resemblance to contemporary depictions of Jesus Christ.

Durer's self-portrait

Raphael's other portraits from his Florentine period included one of his good friend Pietro Bembo, as well as another famous one of Agnolo Doni. Bembo was a Venetian Cardinal and a good friend of Raphael's. It was not unusual for religious figures to have their portraits painted, and with all of his experience Raphael was a natural choice for the task. However, the Bembo portrait, titled *Portrait of Pietro Bembo* (1506), portrays the Venetian Cardinal in somewhat eclectic terms. Instead of the traditional black garb characteristic of a Cardinal, he appears wearing red. Moreover, his face appears extraordinarily similar to that of Raphael in his own self-portrait, as though Raphael had forgotten the identity of his subject. While Raphael's depiction is hardly unflattering — Bembo still possesses soft, beautiful features — the similarity between the portrait and the earlier one Raphael completed of himself is uncanny.

Raphael's portrait of Bembo

The portrait of Doni, known as the *Portrait of Maddalena Doni*, borrows heavily from Leonardo's *Mona Lisa*. Completed between 1505 and 1507, the subject is seated in the same position as the subject of Leonardo's portrait, although she wears a slight scowl instead of the suggestive smile worn by Leonardo's figure. Just as Raphael had portrayed Pietro Perugino with a frown, he applies a similar approach in this work. Instead of portraying his subject in an idealized manner, he conveys her as a relatively unappealing figure, a choice that was presumably made out of a need to depict his subject as realistically as possible. Additionally, while Raphael was undoubtedly influenced by the *Mona Lisa*, he demonstrates a clear disregard for the atmospheric quality of Leonardo's famous work. At a time in which Leonardo and Michelangelo were popularizing the use of naturalistic techniques such as chiaroscuro, Raphael continued to reject naturalistic lighting. Ultimately, the *Portrait of Maddalena Doni* appears as a hybrid between Raphael's earlier portraits (with their Perugino-inspired soft features) and Leonardo's *Mona Lisa*.

Raphael's *Portrait of Maddalena Doni*

    While Raphael completed a select number of famous portraits during his time in Florence, the period is most notable for the numerous Madonna paintings he produced. Unlike his earlier Madonna paintings, the Florentine ones contain the significant difference of portraying the Virgin Mary and baby Jesus in a natural setting. In so doing, Raphael borrowed from the precedent that had been established by Leonardo in his *Virgin of the Rocks* (1483-86), which had been completed roughly 20 years earlier. Through depicting the Madonna in nature, Raphael not only lends her a natural quality but makes her more accessible than if she were positioned in a more fantastical setting. By conveying the Virgin Mary in a realistic environment, he also continued the emphasis on naturalistic Madonna portrayals that he had started while in Perugia.

    A famous example of Raphael's naturalistic Madonnas is *La belle jardinière* (1507). That the title does not make explicit mention of the Virgin Mary alerts the viewer that she is to be viewed similarly to the common woman. Raphael's reworking of the symbolic mother and child archetype also comes through because of the fact that Jesus is not the only young child in the composition; Saint John the Baptist is also shown as an infant. It is also notable that Mary appears as a highly sensual woman. In contrast with the canonical depictions of Christ's mother as pale and somber, the Virgin appears in *La belle jardinière* as a voluptuous and beautiful figure. It is apparent that Raphael intended for her to not only appear as a spiritually pure woman (as evidenced by her familiarity with the natural setting) but also as a desirable (almost lustworthy) woman. In this vein, Frank Roy Fraprie notes that Raphael "brought the Mother of Christ forth from the formal archaicism of medieval pictorial representation, and dared to portray her as a very human, very loving mother who will always touch the hearts of men. He made religious painting naturalistic, and created a Bible in pictures for a world which could not read." (viii). Raphael thus transformed the Virgin Mary from a cold, symbolic figure to a more nurturing woman. He modernized her and created a universal mother that everyone could love.

La belle jardinière

La belle jardinière also reflects the evolution of Raphael's formal technique. Up to this point, he had eschewed the developments in natural lighting that had been made by Leonardo and other noted artists of the Italian Renaissance. However, with *La belle jardinière*, viewers can discern a more diverse array of tonal gradations, including the interplay between light and dark shades. Just as Raphael modernized his archetypal subject matter, he also altered his artistic technique to reflect the developments of the time period.

Another famous Madonna painting of Raphael's was his *Madonna of the Pinks* (1506-07). In an unusual decision, Raphael depicts the Virgin Mary with the baby Jesus in a contemporary interior setting. Since the scene takes place indoors, Raphael is not able to achieve the virtuoso chiaroscuro effects of *La belle jardinière*, but the painting is still remarkable for the extreme detail of the garments worn by Christ's mother. As with Raphael's earlier Madonna portrayals, Mary appears as a voluptuous, sensuous figure, and Christ possesses the soft body of a well cared-for infant. Mary hands the young Jesus a carnation, a well-known symbol for Christ's passion. The painting constitutes an additional example of Raphael's ability to modernize sacred symbols without debasing them, thereby achieving a similar effect to *La belle jardinière*, albeit through different means.

Raphael's *Madonna of the Pinks*

Chapter 4: Life in Rome

Raphael remained in Florence through part of 1508. By this point, he was still only 25 years old, and he showed no signs of getting married and raising a family. This direction was not unusual for artists; Michelangelo never was married either. But Raphael's disregard for family life differed greatly from others. While Michelangelo led an ascetic, monk-like existence that centered almost exclusively around his art, Raphael was a sensualist who was constantly engaged in affairs with young women. Not being tied down to a particular family situation afforded him the easy opportunity to relocate. In 1508, he left for Rome, where he would remain for the rest of his life.

The reasons for Raphael's departure for Rome reflect the grandeur of the ancient city during the early 16th century. Pope Julius II held a deep enthusiasm for the arts and intended to reprise the splendor of ancient Rome. In order to fulfill his ambition, Julius commissioned Raphael to paint the Stanza della Signatura, the papal library in the Vatican. At the same time, Michelangelo was assigned to complete the ceiling of the Sistine Chapel, and Bramante was tasked with designing St. Peter's Cathedral. Through collecting the most premium talent available in Italy, Julius signaled that Rome would be at the forefront of Renaissance art.

A picture of part of the Stanza della Signatura, showing *The Parnassus* (left) and *The School of Athens* (right)

Raphael completed four works for the Stanza della Signatura, and together they comprise the most ambitious project of his career. Each of the works occupies a different wall in the grand library, with one referring to philosophy, one to religion, one to poetry, and one to law.

The first of these was *La Disputa* (1509-10), which portrays the disputation of the sacrament and constitutes the religious wall of the Stanza della Signature. The work is immense in scope, and in many ways, the composition harkens back to Raphael's earliest works completed under Pietro Perugino. The stacking of higher and lower levels recalls altarpieces such as the *Oddi Altarpiece*, and Raphael incorporates the deft symmetry that had surfaced through his early works but had been largely cast aside in the many portraits and Madonna compositions completed during the Florentine period. *La Disputa* is a more mature work than Raphael's earliest works, but it bears a closer similarity to his earliest paintings than the ones he finished while in Florence.

La Disputa

The second component of the Stanza della Signatura, *The School of Athens*, is the most famous and represents the philosophy component of the project. The fresco managed to surpass *La Disputa* and remains Raphael's best-known work. Also completed during 1509 and 1510, the fresco conveys a grand meeting involving many of the greatest minds of Ancient and contemporary Greco-Roman society. The two figures at the center of the frame are Aristotle and Plato, but the symmetrical barrier drawn between the two figures is of particular significance. This was meant to reflect the fact that while Aristotle represents a scientific intellectual approach, Plato adopts a more philosophical, less mathematically rigorous methodology. Accordingly, the figures on the side of Aristotle are more scientifically-oriented, while those flanking Plato are more intangible in their intellectual approaches. Considering his interest in symmetry and mathematical accuracy, it should come as no surprise that Raphael includes himself in the camp of Aristotle. Ultimately, *The School of Athens* not only stands as arguably Raphael's greatest technological accomplishment but also an impressive example of narrative painting. Raphael's technique applies the principles of symmetry and perspective and adopts them on a massive scale, but the rich thematic message constitutes a sophisticated explanation of the principles of humanistic thought associated with contemporary society in Rome.

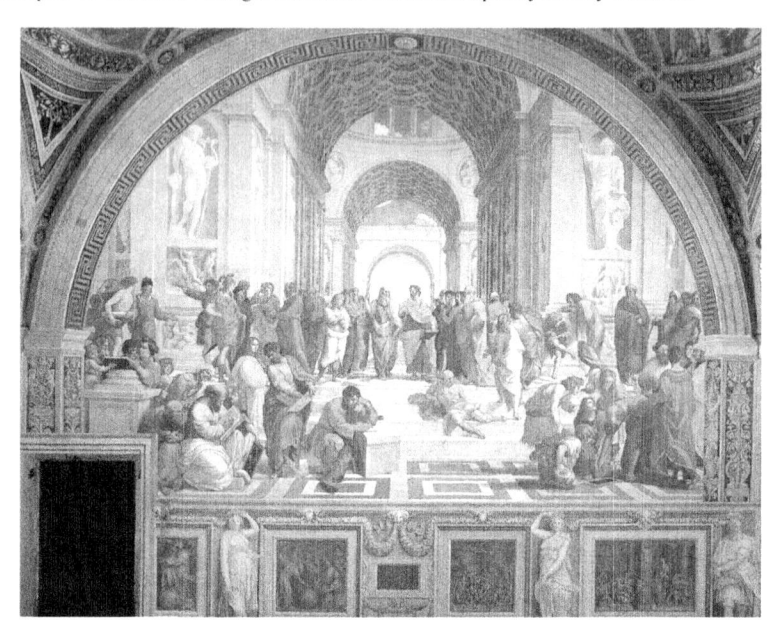

The School of Athens

The final two walls of the papal library are less impressive than *La Disputa* or *The School of Athens* but still remarkable in their own right. Comprising the poetic wall of the library, *The Parnassus* (1511) conveys Apollo and his Muses surrounded by a collection of famous poets. The natural setting recalls the landscapes associated with Raphael's Florentine paintings, but the scale is far grander. As with the other walls of the library, Raphael maintains a strict devotion to symmetry, with Apollo dividing the image at the center in a manner that suggests Raphael's early crucifixion altarpieces.

The Parnassus

The judicial wall of the Stanza della Signatura, *The Cardinal Virtues* (1511) is the smallest in scope and depicts the cardinal virtues of fortitude, temperance, and prudence. The fresco is interrupted at its center by the entrance to the room, and as a result the symmetry of the designs is somewhat disrupted. Even still, *The Cardinal Virtues* remains a dramatic composition that is both technically impressive and thematically important.

The Cardinal Virtues

Taken together, the four walls of the Stanza della Signatura easily comprise Raphael's most monumental achievement. The immense scope of the project makes it Raphael's answer to Michelangelo's *Sistine Chapel*, and while the work is perhaps not as revolutionary as the more famous Michelangelo's work, it stands as a fine achievement on its own. While the Sistine Chapel Ceiling is heavily subversive, thanks to its substantial amount of nudity and veiled subtexts, Raphael adopted a more measured approach that referenced the major philosophical and artistic currents of the time period. The four walls demonstrate a balanced approach to the technical and philosophical currents of Renaissance Italy, balancing the sacred with the secular in a more subtle manner than any of Raphael's contemporaries.

After completing the walls of the Stanza della Signatura, Raphael settled into life in Rome. He had worked at the Vatican since his arrival in 1508, and with the completion of the library in 1511, he was finally afforded the opportunity to administer a proper workshop, much as Pietro Perugino himself had done years earlier in Perugia. Over the next 9 years and up until his death, Raphael and his students would complete an immense number of paintings, spanning from portraiture to more narrative-based compositions. Thus, this chapter of his life involved not just the production of some of his most famous works but also his evolution into a teacher.

Among the portraits completed by Raphael and his students during the last decade of his life were his *Portrait of Pope Julius II* (1511-12), *Portrait of Bindo Altoviti* (1514), and *La Fornarina* (1518). The *Portrait of Pope Julius II* is likely the most famous, portraying the pope in the final years before his passing. Though it was completed years later, the work bears important similarities with Raphael's early portrait of Perugino, especially the choice to depict his famous subject in a manner less than attractive. Pope Julius II appears weary and helpless, though it could be said his contemplative face reflects a dignity and respect between Raphael and his patron. Perhaps because the pope was advanced in age, the subject does not possess the beauty that characterizes Raphael's other subjects, but his technique still manages to portray the pope in sympathetic (if not beautiful) terms.

Portrait of Pope Julius II

Raphael's *Portrait of Bindo Altoviti* is more commensurate with Raphael's style of portraiture. The subject possesses the soft features and almost feminine quality of Raphael's earlier works. The similarity between *Portrait of Bindo Altoviti* and works such as *Portrait of Pietro Bembo* make it difficult to believe that the painting was not originally attributed to Raphael (Brown and Nimmen). It is also important to note that Bindo Altoviti was a banker and not a religious figure, another example of the secularization of painting and the fact that artists were respected social figures who were not solely dependent on church commissions or royal patrons. One of the most curious aspects of the painting is that Altoviti's face appears similar to that of Raphael, continuing a trend that had developed in Raphael's Florentine portraits. It's yet another example of how Raphael's portraits seem to include a degree of self-portraiture.

Portrait of Bindo Altoviti

    La Fornarina was Raphael's final portrait, and it depicts his famous mistress. Raphael was a passionate man who engaged in numerous affairs throughout his young life, and the subject of *La Fornarina* is the most famous among his mistresses. In the portrait, she appears with the soft features that characterize his earlier subjects. Moreover, Raphael applies the veiled sexuality that surfaced through his Madonnas and renders it more explicitly. The subject does not appear ashamed to bare her breasts, and her smile suggests an almost lascivious pleasure in the act. Because the portrait was completed at the end of his career, it is impossible to determine which direction Raphael's style would have taken, but *La Fornarina* suggests that he would have incorporated more sexually suggestive subject matter.

La Fornarina

    The most ambitious paintings completed by Raphael during the final decade of his life were the *Raphael Cartoons*, a series of 10 tapestries completed for Pope Leo X between 1515-16. The cartoons portray scenes from the Bible, and they were hung below Michelangelo's Sistine Chapel Ceiling art in the Vatican. The contrast between the two Renaissance masters is as notable as ever when comparing the works. Michelangelo's figures are dynamic, while Raphael's are more solid and monumental, and though the scenes are relatively banal, Kleinbub notes that Raphael's characters are nonetheless invested with profound spirituality (41). The gravitas of his subjects heightens their spiritual resonance, making the tapestries perhaps more appropriate for the religious setting than Michelangelo's famous work.

Saint Paul Preaching in Athens. **This is one of** ***Raphael's Cartoons***

    A significant development that occurred during Raphael's period in Rome was that he began designing architecture. He designed the Palazzo Aquila and the Villa Madama, perfecting a monumental, mathematically-informed style that cohered with the spirit of the High Renaissance. His most famous architectural design began in 1514. Following the death of Bramante, he was appointed head architect for the redesign of Saint Peter's Cathedral in Rome, due to the fact Bramante had named him successor. On August 1, 1514, Raphael received the following instructions:

> "It is of the utmost importance for the work on the Roman temple of the Prince of the Apostles [St. Peter's], that the stones and marble, of which a great quantity are needed, be easily obtained in the neighborhood rather than imported from afar. And since we know that the Roman ruins provide them abundantly, and that all sorts of stones are found by almost anybody who starts to build in or around Rome, or digs up the ground for some other reason, we create you, because we have entrusted you with the direction of the work, inspector in chief of all the marble and all the stone which will be excavated from now on within Rome or within ten miles around it, so that you can purchase them if they are modest, and low origin and rank, that they should first of all inform you, in your position as head superviser, of all the marble and stones of all kinds discovered in the above-mentioned precincts. Whoever will not have complied within three days will be punishable by a 100 to 300 gold ducats fine, as you should decide. Since we have been informed that masons unheedingly cut and use ancient pieces of marble and stone that bear inscriptions or other remains which often contain things

memorable, and which deserve to be preserved for the progress of classical studies and the elegance of the Latin tongue, but that get lost in this fashion, we order all stone quarries of Rome not to break or saw stones bearing inscriptions without your order and permission, liable to the same fine if they disobey our orders."

Ironically, Raphael would not complete the design, and today Bramante and Michelangelo are better remembered for their contributions more than Raphael. Still, he brought significant changes to the design, including adding large piers throughout the nave. His design was far grander than that of Bramante, and he emphasized the importance of being able to adequately view the cathedral from any vantage point (Lotz). In so doing, Raphael enhanced the monumentality of St. Peter's, making the building more squarely in the tradition of antiquity.

The last ambitious project by Raphael was *Transfiguration*, which was commissioned to serve as the altarpiece for the Narbonne Cathedral in France. Raphael never completed the project, which he worked on from 1517 until his death three years later. *Transfiguration* is an interesting work, because it is both iconoclastic yet still reflective of Raphael's other works. Completing an altarpiece brought him full-circle with the altarpieces he had completed under Perugino early in his career, and the vertically organized composition recalled the style of his early altarpieces. At the same time, the highly saturated colors and extremely dramatic postures contrast with Raphael's characteristically monumental style, gesturing toward the melodramatic, Mannerist style of Michelangelo. In this regard, *Transfiguration* also reflects the passing of the Renaissance and anticipates the arrival of Mannerism, which would emerge in full force over the course of the following decade.

Transfiguration

By 1520, Raphael was at the height of his fame and was viewed as the equal to Leonardo and Michelangelo. However, his life ended prematurely on April 6 of that year, when he was just 37 years old. The causes for his death remain unclear. For a long time, accounts of his death had attributed it to sexual intercourse with one of his mistresses. While the story is almost certainly apocryphal, it reflects the passionate sensibility of Raphael, a quality that separated him from Michelangelo and other famous artists of the period. All that is known for sure is that he contracted an illness that only took two weeks to kill him, and his impending death seemed so certain that he spent his final days preparing a will.

When the Italian Renaissance is discussed, Raphael is not typically remembered as favorably as Leonardo or Michelangelo. However, in many ways, Raphael is the Renaissance artist *par excellence*. While Michelangelo often subverted the formal and thematic norms of the time period and Leonardo disregarded the spiritual, Raphael synthesized the scientific and the spiritual and garnered a level of mass appeal that managed to surpass that of his contemporaries. After his death there was a frenzied attempt to document and commemorate his life, effectively inaugurating the genre of the artist biography (Lathers). To this end, while it is true that Raphael's artwork has not aged as well as his rivals, it is best appreciated when placed in the context of his time period.

To some degree, it's fitting that Raphael's work occasionally mirrored his artistic rivals while also standing alone. The Renaissance's 3 most famous artists have been permanently associated and compared with each other, and the sparse details of certain parts of their lives has given rise to speculation over the relationships they had with each other. Vasari referenced a rivalry bordering on animosity between Michelangelo and Leonardo, and he also recounted an anecdote that said Raphael was able to get a sneak peek of Michelangelo's work on the Sistine Chapel and changed his own depiction of Isaiah in response. When Michelangelo saw the similarities in the stances of his Isaiah and Raphael's, he was enraged. According to Vasari, he was convinced "that Bramante had deliberately done him that wrong for the sake of Raphael's reputation and benefit." Vasari even claimed that whenever Michelangelo heard someone praise Raphael, he would respond, "Everything he knew he learned from me."

Bramante

Vasari was full of praise for both men, but he countered Michelangelo's allegation, writing, "What [Raphael] had seen of Michelangelo's paintings enabled him to give his own style more majesty and grandeur…Nevertheless, Raphael realized that in this matter he could never rival the accomplishments of Michelangelo, and therefore, like the judicious man he was….he resolved to emulate and perhaps surpass him in other respects….He decided not to waste his time by imitating Michelangelo's style but to attain a catholic excellence in the other fields of painting."

Furthermore, Raphael's career should also be recognized for the contributions he made to the profession of the artist. His success in the field of portraiture reflects the ability for the artist to make a living without relying on the church, and he also exemplified the rise of the artist as a worldly individual with prestigious standing in society (Hulse). Regardless of the abbreviated tenure of his career, he left behind a career of immense scope, spanning several painting genres and architecture, and his life exemplified the true spirit of the Renaissance as an artistic and intellectual movement.

Bibliography

Bossy, Michel-Andre, Thomas Brothers, and John C. McEnroe. *Artists, Writers, and Musicians: An Encyclopedia of People Who Changed the World*. New York: The Oryx Press, 2001.

Brown, David, and Jane Van Nimmen. *Raphael and the Beautiful Banker: The Story of the Bindo Altoviti Portrait*. New Haven: Yale University Press, 2005.

Fraprie, Frank R. *The Raphael Book: An Account of the Life of Raphael Santi of Urbino and his place in the Development of Art, together with a description of his Paintings and Frescos*. Boston: The Colonial Press, 1912.

Goffen, Roma. *Renaissance Rivals: Michelangelo, Leonardo, Raphael*. New Haven: Yale University Press, 2004.

Hulse, Clark. *The Rule of Art: Literature and Painting in the Renaissance*. Chicago: University of Chicago Press, 1990.

Janson, Horst W., and Anthony F. Janson. *History of Art: The Western Tradition: Slipcase*. Upper Saddle River: 2004.

Kleinbub, Christian K. *Vision and the Visionary in Raphael*. University Park: The Pennsylvania State University Press, 2011.

Lathers, Marie. *Bodies of Art: French Literary Realism and the Artist's Model*. Lincoln: University of Nebraska Press, 2001.

Lotz, Wolfgang. *Architecture in Italy: 1500-1600*. New Haven: Yale University Press, 1995.

McCurdy, Edward. *Raphael Santi*. Charleston: Nabu Press, 2010.

Strinati, Claudio. *Raphael*. Milano: Giunti Editore, 1998.

Sweetser, Moses F. *Raphael*. Charleston: BiblioLife Press, 2009.

Printed in Great Britain
by Amazon